Seeing!

Join the crowd and start *Seeing!* For artists, both young and old, consider this an art education workbook. As you make your way through the puzzles, you'll be building the visual skills every artist needs. For puzzle lovers, here's an activity book unlike the rest. For folks who aren't ready to retire their brains just because they may no longer be employed, take up the oboe...*or* take up this book. Isn't it time to start seeing what you've been missing?

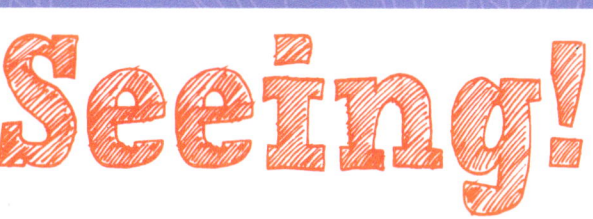

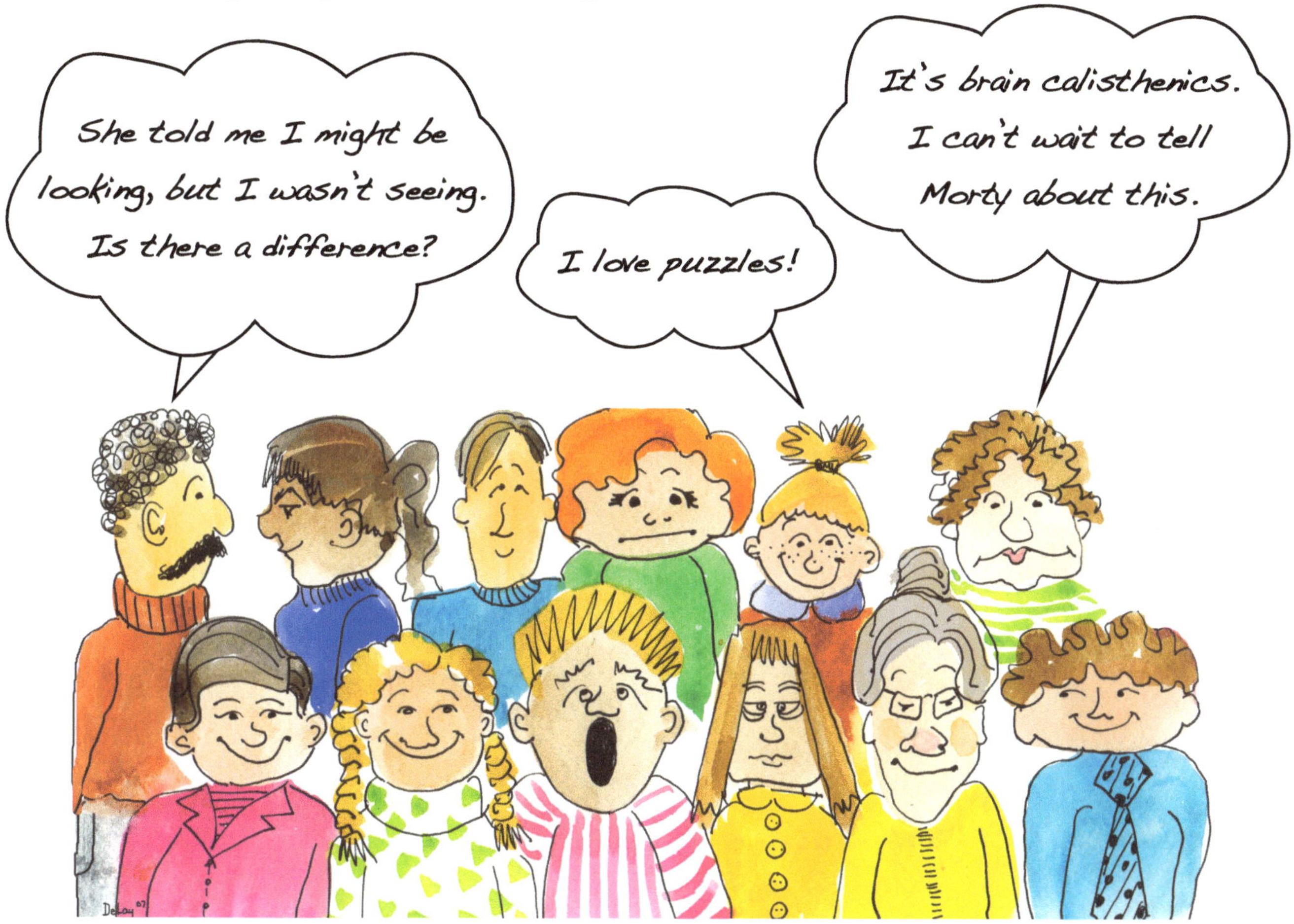

Elizabeth DeLay Jurkowski

About the Author

Elizabeth DeLay Jurkowski, like most artists, began with drawing and, although she has dabbled in many different media and styles, pastel portraiture has always been where her heart and her gift meet. Elizabeth thought she would be a public school art teacher but, after graduating from college with a teaching certificate, her career went in a different direction. She sold Macintosh computers. Then, when artists started to use computers to create, she taught them how to use the software they needed. Throughout her career she has never stopped being an artist, doing commissioned portraits when time allowed. She taught the occasional evening drawing class during the time her children were growing up but it wasn't until later in life that she was drawn back to her art education roots. In 2003 she created an after-school art program for children and has been enthusiastically teaching youngsters to draw ever since.

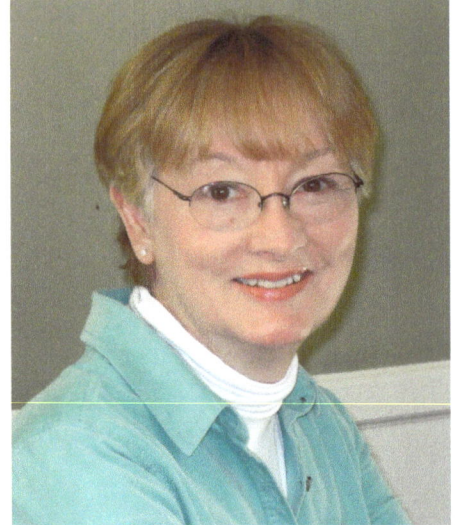

Seeing! Copyright © 2013 by Elizabeth DeLay Jurkowski
ISBN-13: 978-1493662760
ISBN-10: 1493662767

Printed by CreateSpace, An Amazon.com Company
Available from Amazon.com and other book stores

Introduction

Seeing Like an Artist

Artists see things differently. That is to say, they process visual information differently. Learning to see more like an artist will improve your ability to draw accurately, no matter what your skill level might be. But this ability is, in no way, meant only for artistic people. We can all develop our observational skills the way artists have. What it takes is a willingness to explore a different way of paying attention to what our eyes take in.

Normally the act of seeing happens very quickly and without our having to think about it. In an instant our eyes have sent the message to the brain and the brain has interpreted it. Unfortunately, our pre-conceived ideas of what we know get in the way and lead us to see only what we expect to see. But we can bypass that natural tendency and process the visual information unencumbered. Artists do it everyday and everyone can learn the same skills. The old adage suggests that if we want to enjoy life more, we need to "wake up and smell the roses." Imagine how much more interesting life would seem if we decided to slow down and actually see the roses in all their glory. When you train your artist eye, life will become a juicier visual experience.

I am an art teacher as well as a portrait artist. When I was young, I wasn't aware of how I managed to draw accurately. It was just something I did without thinking. But then I read the classic, *Drawing on the Right Side of the Brain*, and I had a proverbial "ah-ha" experience. Author Betty Edwards described specific perceiving skills that facilitated accurate drawing. She was describing what I had always done—but unconsciously. Becoming aware that drawing was more about careful observation than anything else, changed my teaching forever. I began to teach drawing from the perspective of seeing better. I'm convinced that I have so many success stories because I teach my students observational skills rather than "how to draw." As my students become better at seeing they also become better at drawing.

Paying Attention

When an artist works from life or from a photo, and his goal is to draw accurately, he puts his attention to work in some very specific ways. He looks at, and carefully compares, what he sees in the subject before him with his drawing as it develops. Artists become very good at noticing the differences between the two. The fewer differences they see, the more accurate they know their drawing is. Some people are born with a keen ability to notice differences but just as many have learned the skill along the way. Of course, you already notice differences but how discerning are you? It isn't difficult to improve your skills, in fact, using this book will make it fun.

You may notice that the puzzles in *Seeing!* are similar to other activity books you're familiar with. The puzzles, for the most part, center around finding differences and deciding which things match. But, my exercises were originally created for art students so all the subject matter is art based. What I came to realize over the years was that core observational skills were the same for everyone. My art oriented puzzles were not good just for developing artists. They could help everyone to improve their visual perceiving skills.

The puzzles in this book are meant to be fun but they have also been designed to develop specific skills. At the beginning it might feel strange to concentrate so hard on seeing but you'll find that the more you use these skills, in a conscious way, the more natural it will become. Soon you'll just apply them automatically and won't need to think about them at all. That's about the time you'll discover your world holds so many things you hadn't noticed before and your visual perception will never be the same again.

How To

No Drawing Skill Needed

This is not a drawing instruction book. Your success does not require any drawing skill. The activities are equally appropriate for artists and non-artists alike, so please don't let performance anxiety get in your way. There are some exercises in which you will be asked to copy a line drawing but they are more about observing and replicating relationships than drawing well. If, upon completing one of the *Draw It* exercises, you don't think your drawing looks right, use that opportunity to practice better seeing by finding and correcting the differences between your drawing and mine.

Level of Difficulty

Each puzzle has a level of difficulty designation. It's there to prevent you from getting discouraged by attempting more difficult puzzles before you get the hang of how everything works. Noticing the very subtle details of the more difficult puzzles will become easier as your observation skills grow. Getting frustrated would kill the fun so please begin with the easy ones and work your way up to the most difficult.

Slow Down!

This is the most important instruction. You cannot train your eye if you won't slow down to observe carefully. Many of the differences you'll be expected to notice will not be obvious and you'll miss them if you're in a hurry. If you're someone who habitually speeds through everything, this will be a challenge. Try to let go of the hurry mode and clear your mind of distracting thoughts. Allow yourself to get immersed in the details of the picture and you'll find it becomes a surprisingly meditative experience.

When you're comparing two pictures, scan from one to the other, over and over. As your observational skills improve you'll get better and better at catching things but it takes time and patience.

Answers

The puzzle solutions are shown at the back of the book. If you find you're having trouble with a puzzle, you'll probably be tempted to peak at the solution but don't. Training your eye takes practice, so instead of giving in, go on to another and come back later. Knowing the answers won't grow your brain, but struggling to figure it out will.

There are nine differences in the bottom line drawing. Concentrate only on the lines of the squirrel and the feeder. The grid lines you see are only there to help you notice and compare things. Be sure you look back and forth over and over to catch all of the differences and don't hurry.

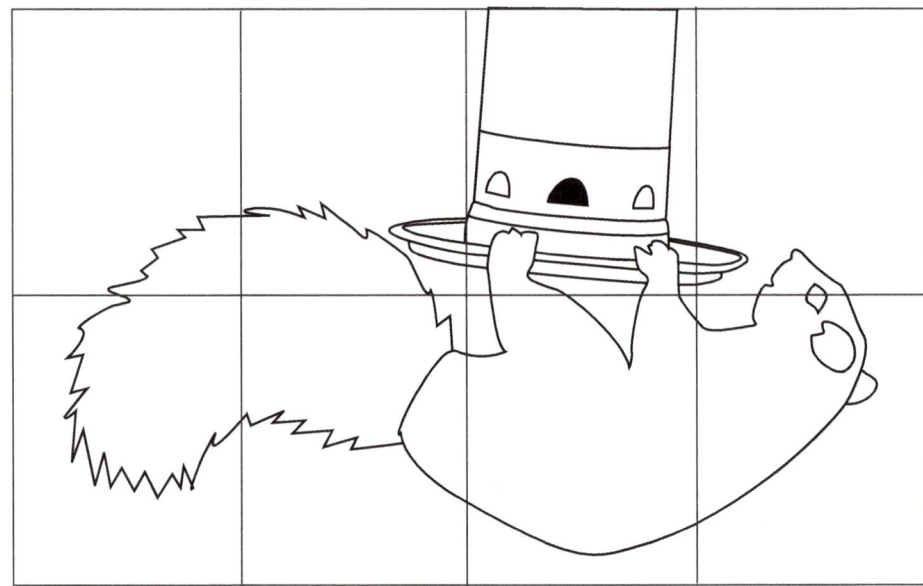

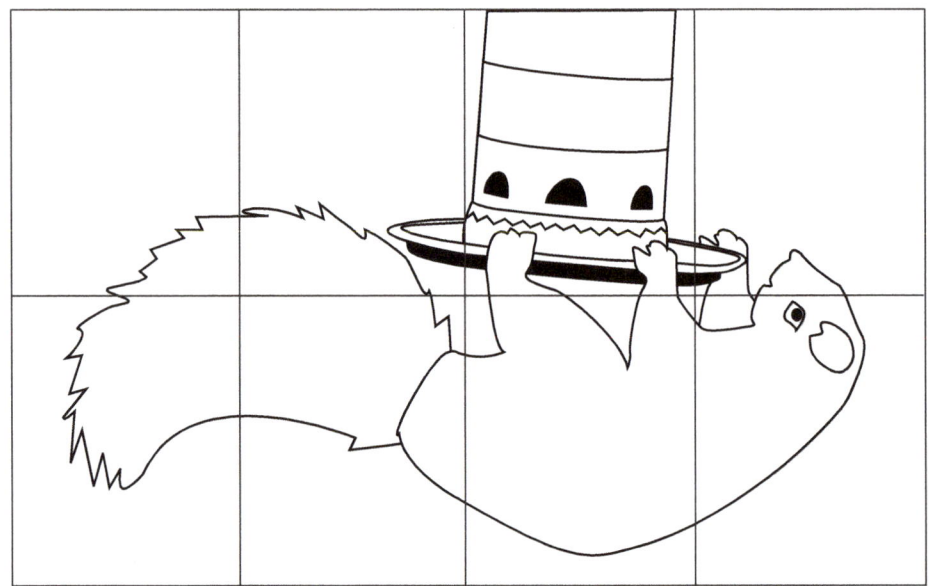

Look for nine changes that have been made to the bottom drawing. See if you can find all nine. The grid lines are not part of the puzzle. They are there to help you notice and compare things. You'll need to look back and forth over and over to catch some of the small differences. If you're having difficulty, it might help you to compare only one pair of the eight grid boxes at a time.

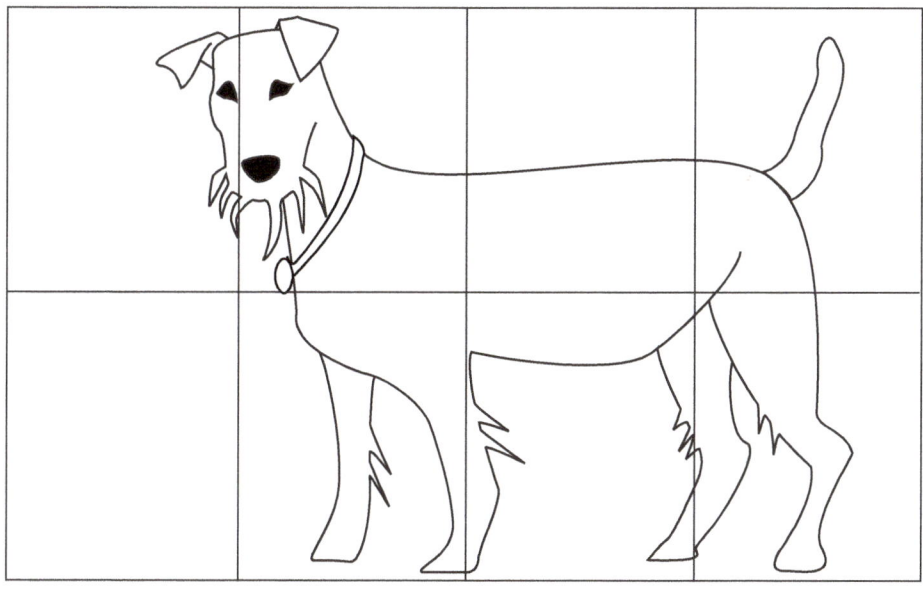

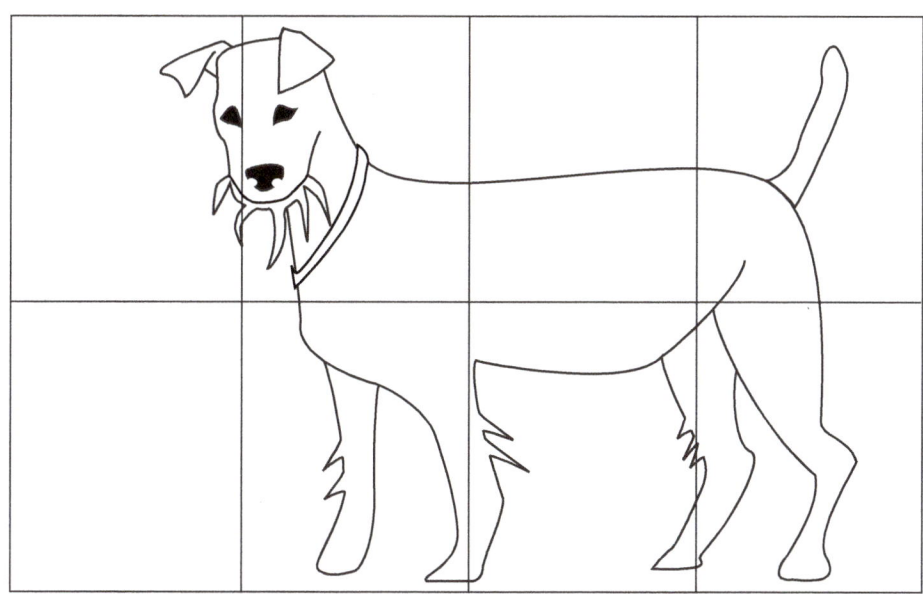

This is Ronnie the rooster. He is made up of seven shapes. If any of the shapes were different, it wouldn't be Ronnie. From the many shapes on the next page, pick out the pieces that you would need to make an exact replica of Ronnie. You may think this looks easy and want to speed through choosing but better seeing takes more time. Slow yourself down and look carefully. There are only seven of the right shapes and many that are wrong. Which ones match the real Ronnie? Circle your choices or make of list of them on a separate piece of paper.

Ronnie

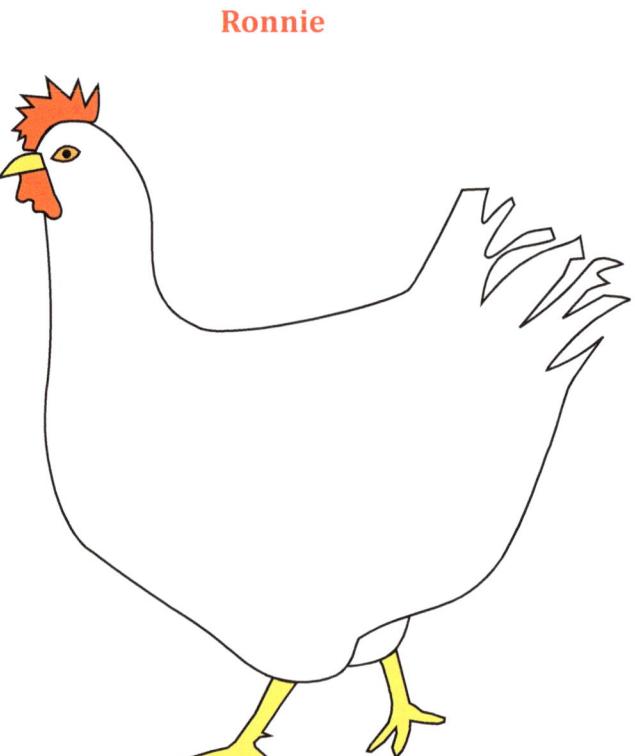

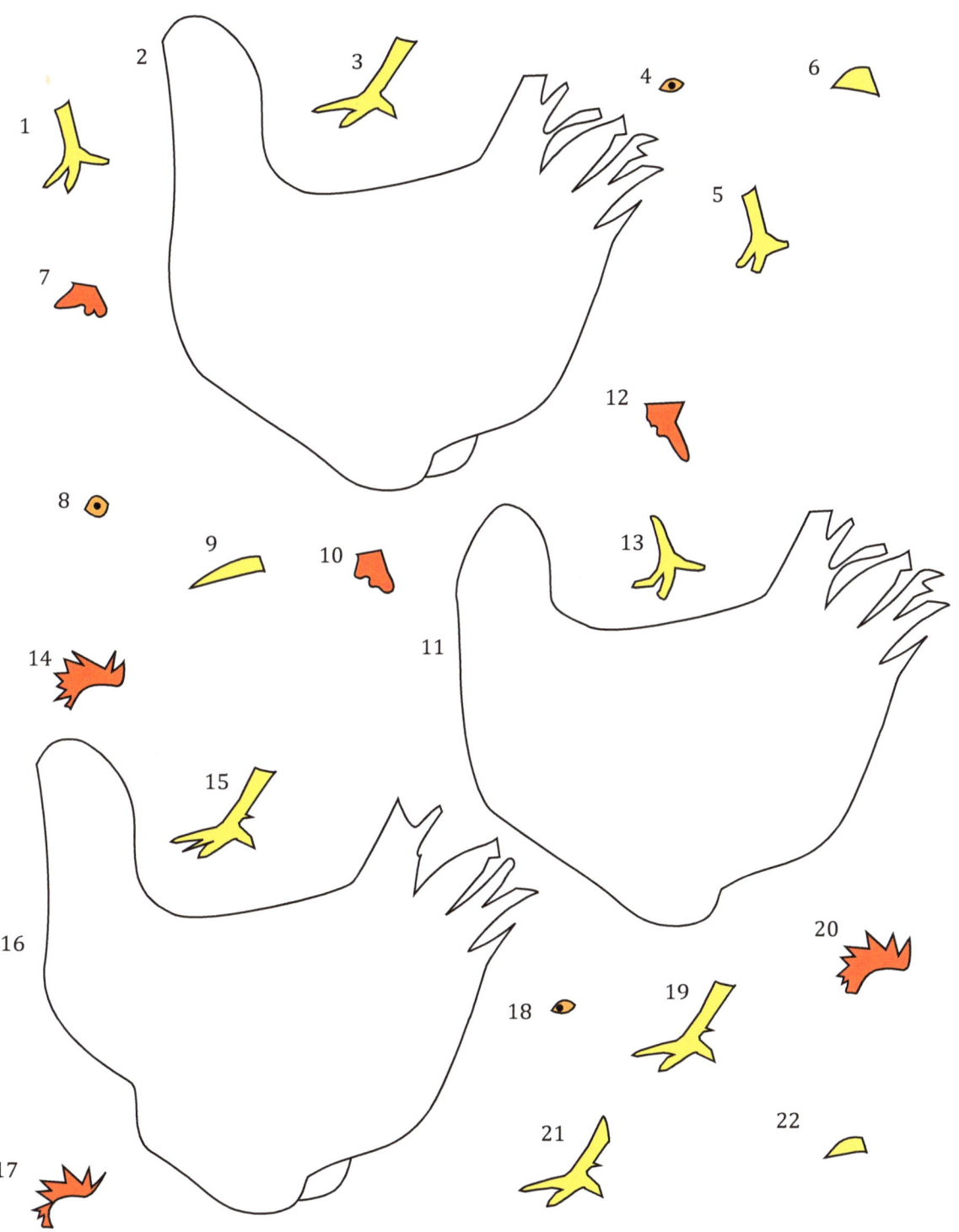

9

Using a pencil, copy the red line into the lower box. Try to make your lines fit the boxes in exactly the same way. Pay attention to how close lines are to edges and where they cross over the grid lines. If you have trouble with the curves, notice the shape of the space outside the curve and make yours match. Don't hurry. Look, study, compare—THEN begin to draw. During the drawing process, continue to look back at the original to compare your progress.

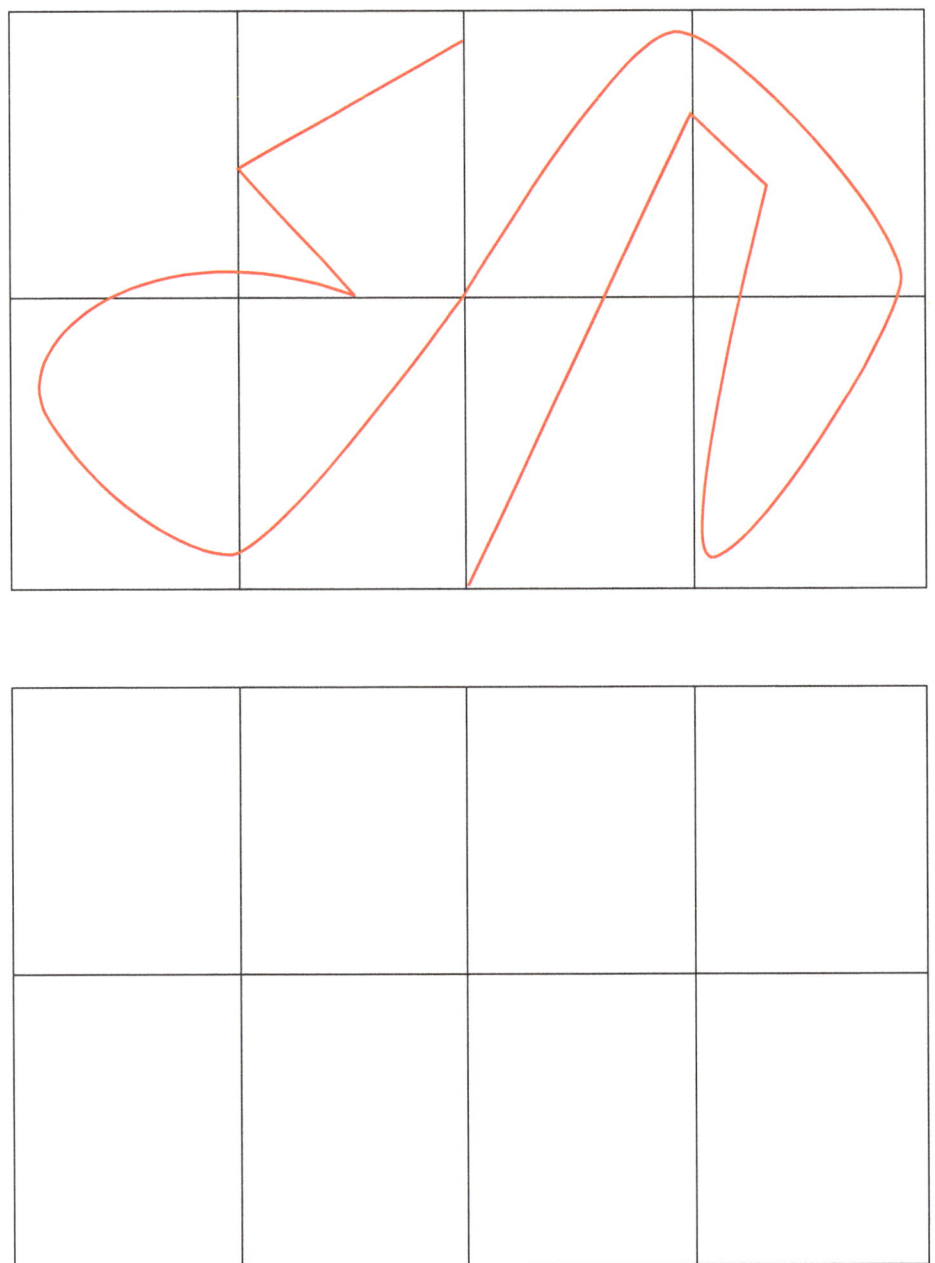

Look for the ways the bottom set of bottles have been changed from the top set. The closer you can come to finding all eight, the better your artist eye is becoming. It isn't enough to see that a bottle is just different. You need to notice exactly what the differences are. There might be more than one difference in a bottle. If you can't find all eight, come back later and try again. Pay attention to bottle color, spacing and tilt, as well as to any changes in the basic shape.

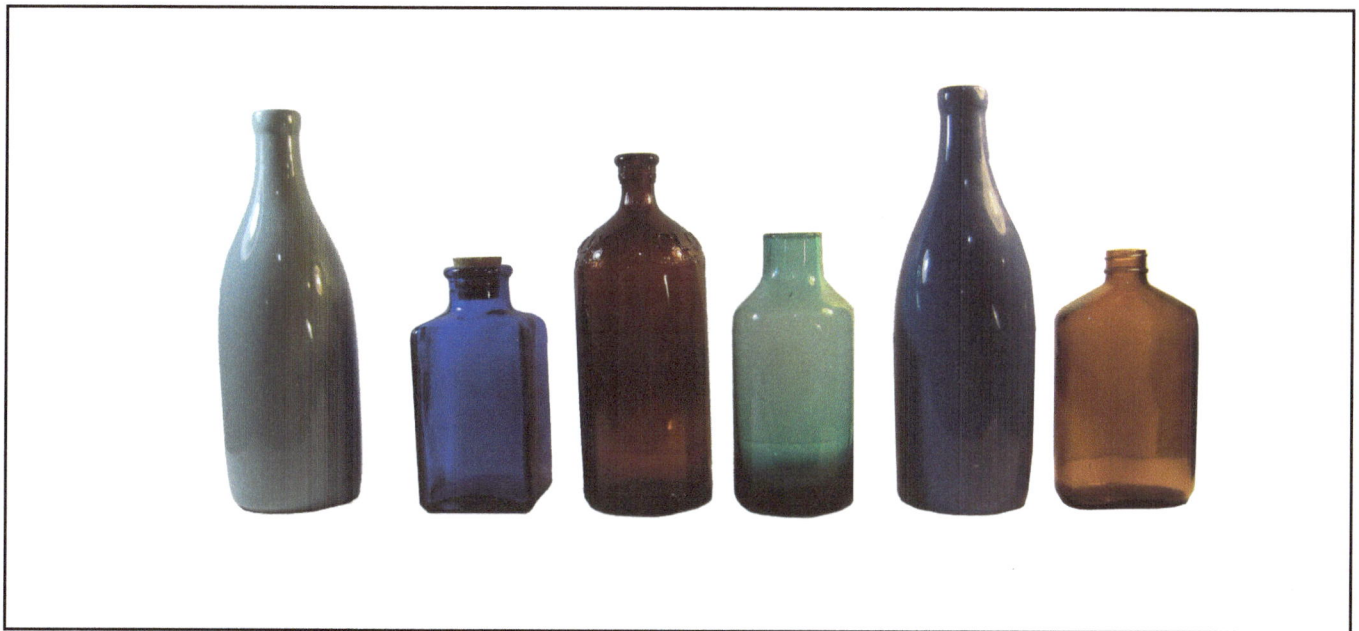

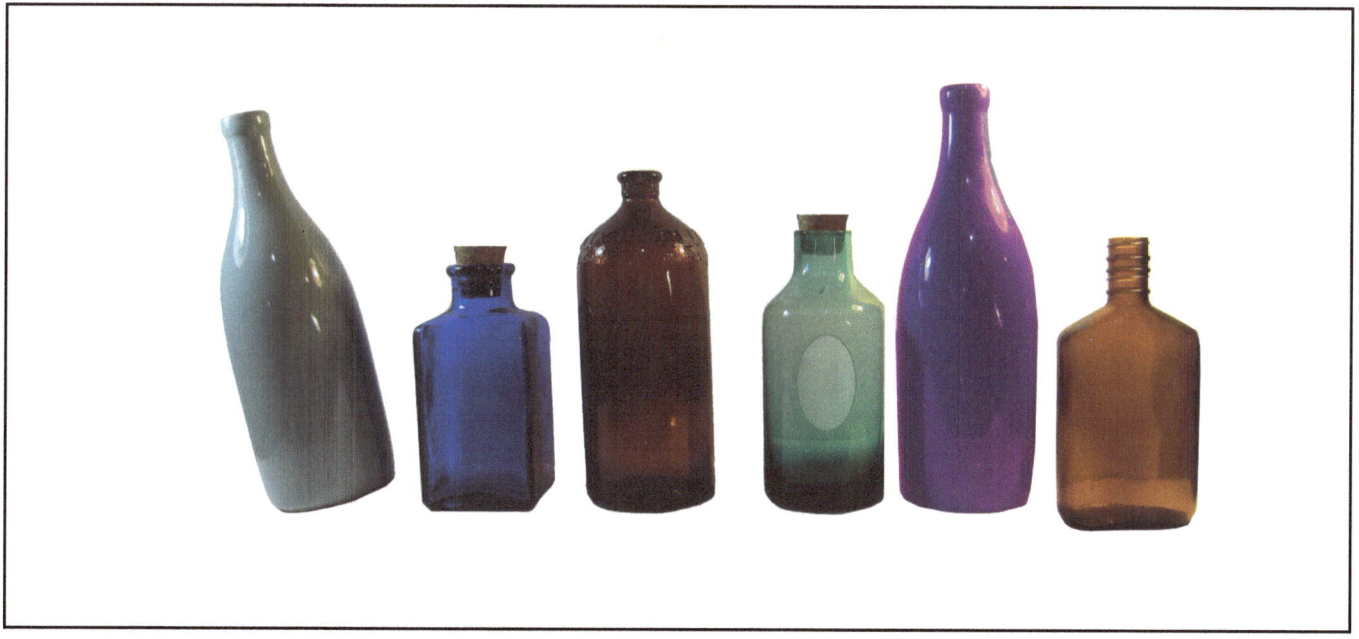

Imagine that this horse picture is a jigsaw puzzle and the brown horse is the largest piece of the puzzle. Your job is to identify all the other pieces. You will have to look carefully and decide which eight pieces on the following page are the correct shapes of the background puzzle pieces.

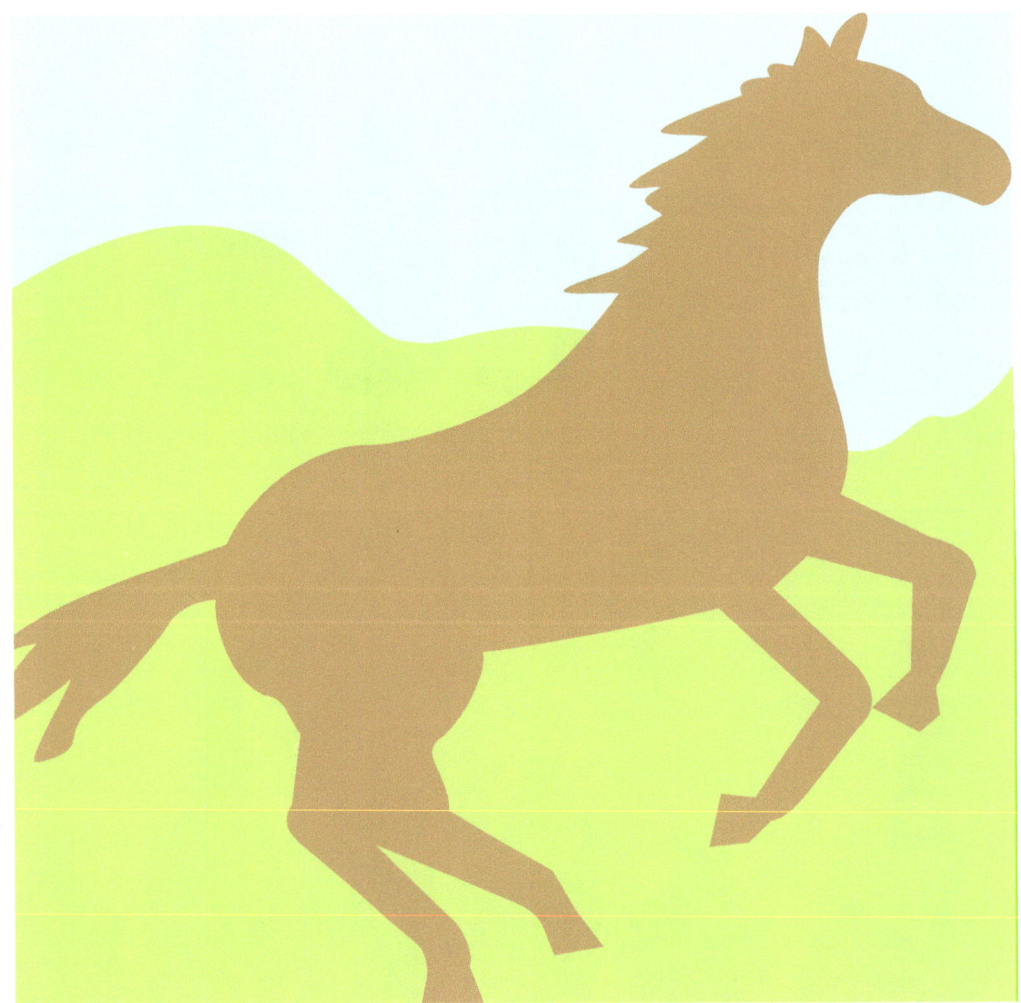

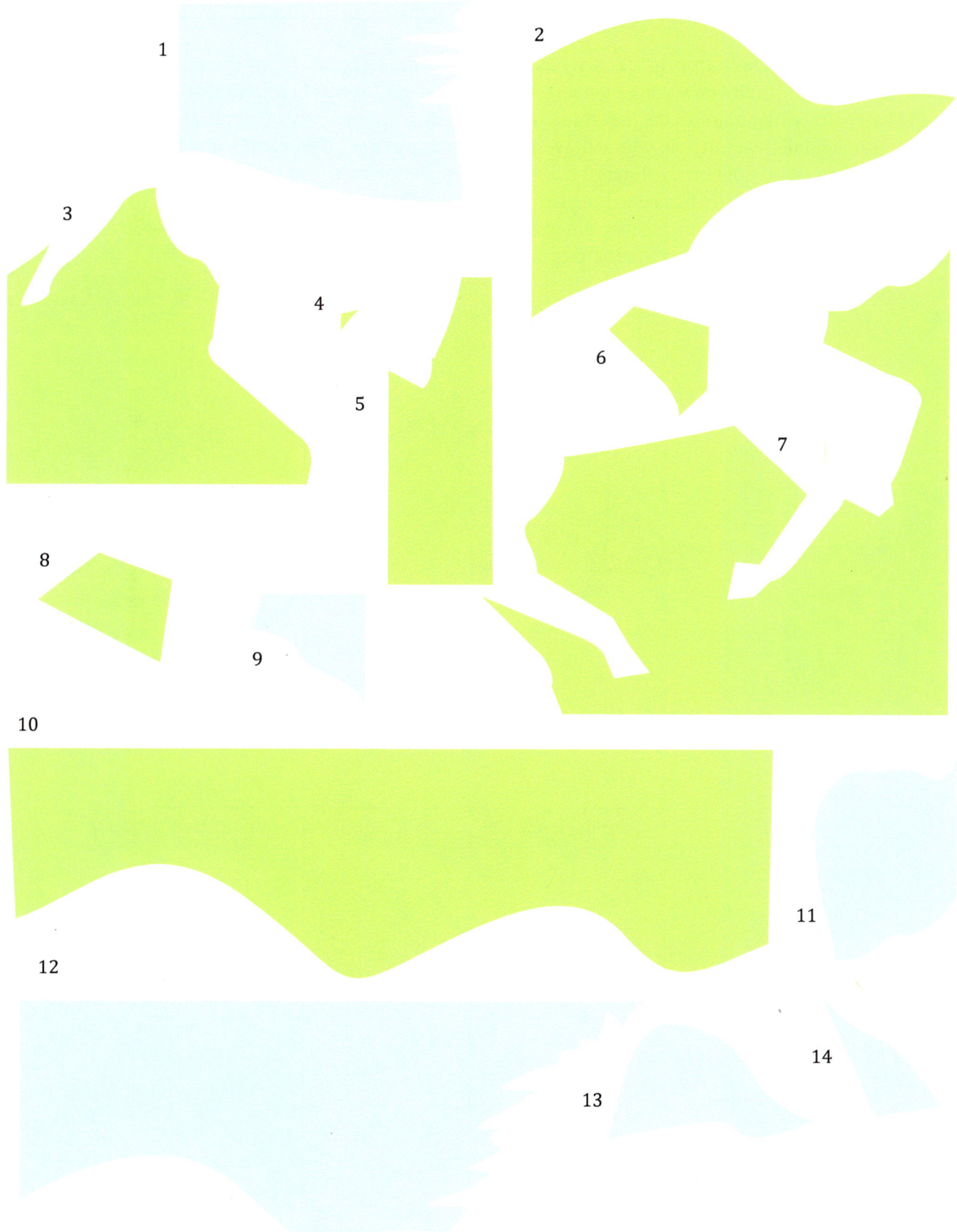

1

2

3

4

5

6

7

8

9

10

11

12

13

14

13

Draw the umbrella in the bottom grid exactly as you see it in the top grid. If your lines fit the boxes in precisely the same way, then you'll know you're getting it right. Don't get lazy and just draw any old umbrella. In fact, forget you're drawing an umbrella. Just think about drawing a set of curvy lines that are just like the curvy lines of the original. It would help you to draw a more accurate curve if you had some helper marks. For each curve draw two small dots on the lower grid, one where the curve starts and another where it ends. Make sure your dots are accurately placed in the grid. Now look at the path you'll need to follow to make the appropriate line. In your imagination, go over the path a few more times before you actually draw it. It seems that practicing with an imaginary line first helps get curves right.

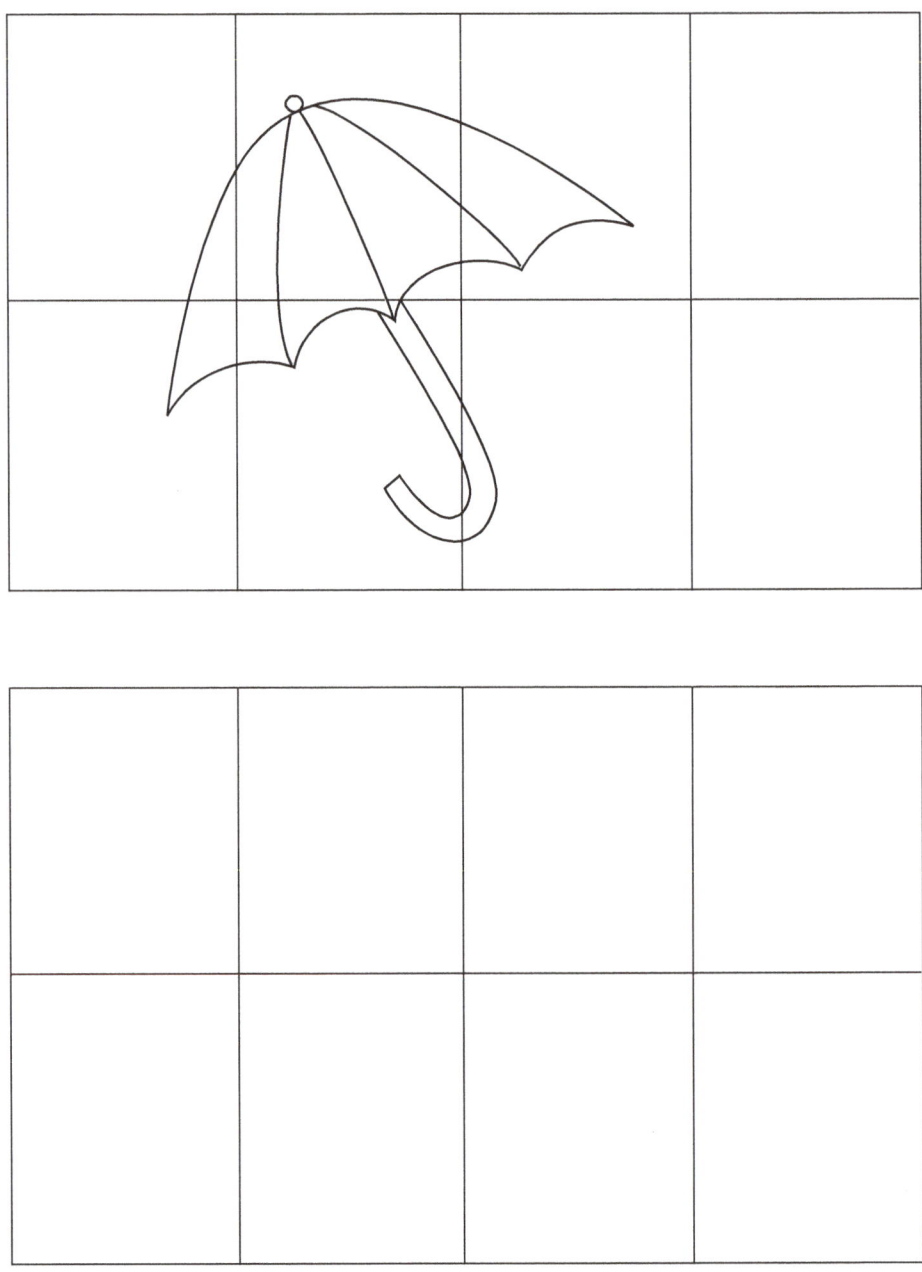

There are 13 changes that have been made to *drawing 2*. Take your time and try to find all 13 before you look up the answer. Keep looking back and forth between the two drawings until you notice all the changes.

drawing 1

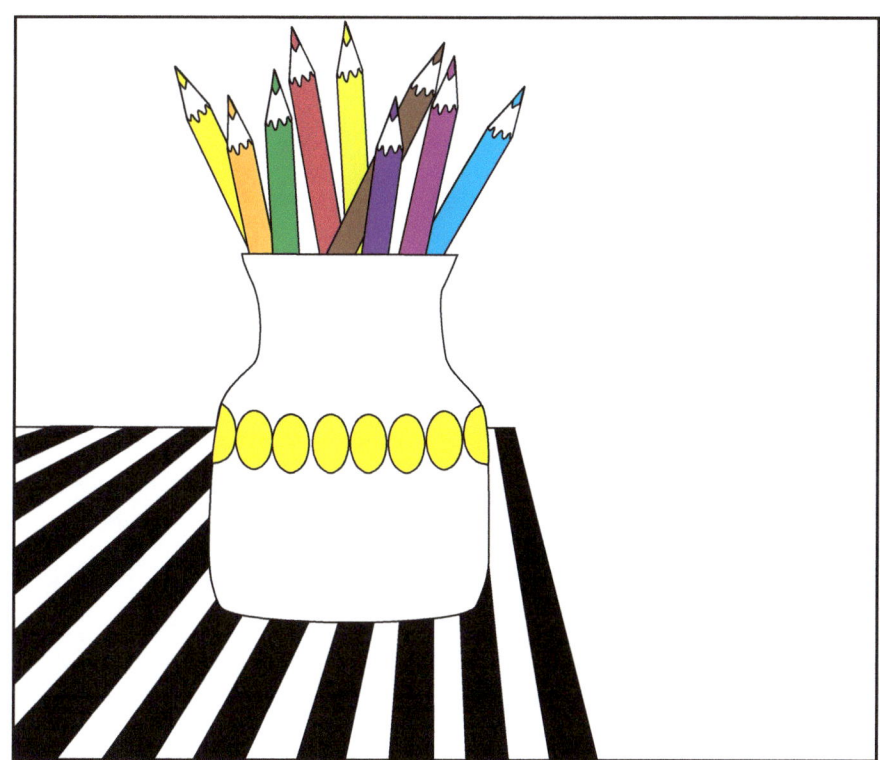

drawing 2

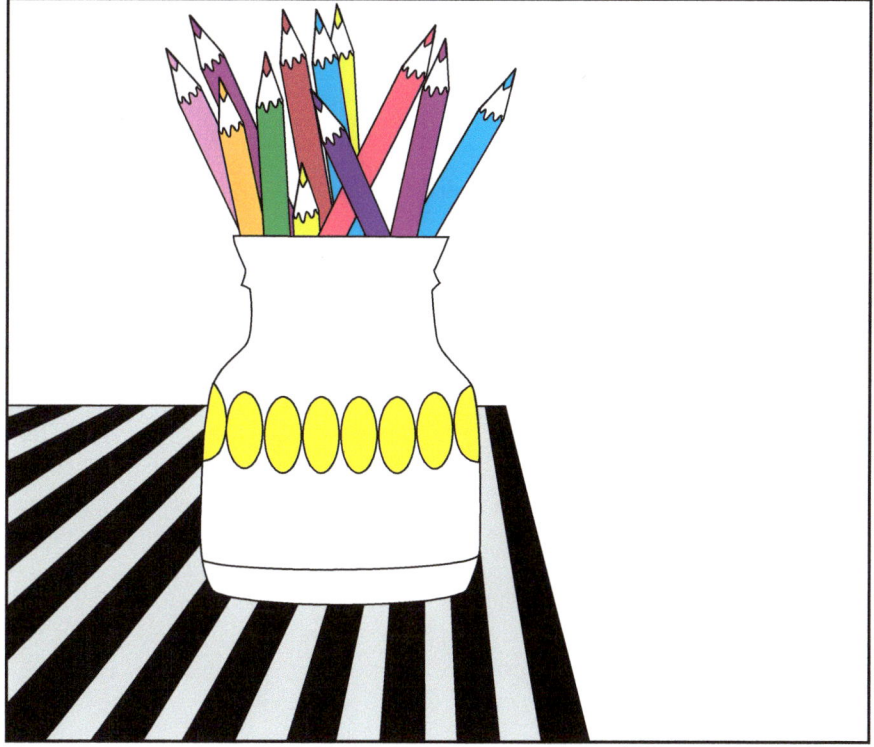

Carefully compare the set of cartoon faces on this page with the set on the following page. There are 15 changes that have been made to the faces in *group 2*. Can you spot all 15? On a separate piece of paper, make a list of the ones you find so you can more easily keep track.

group 1

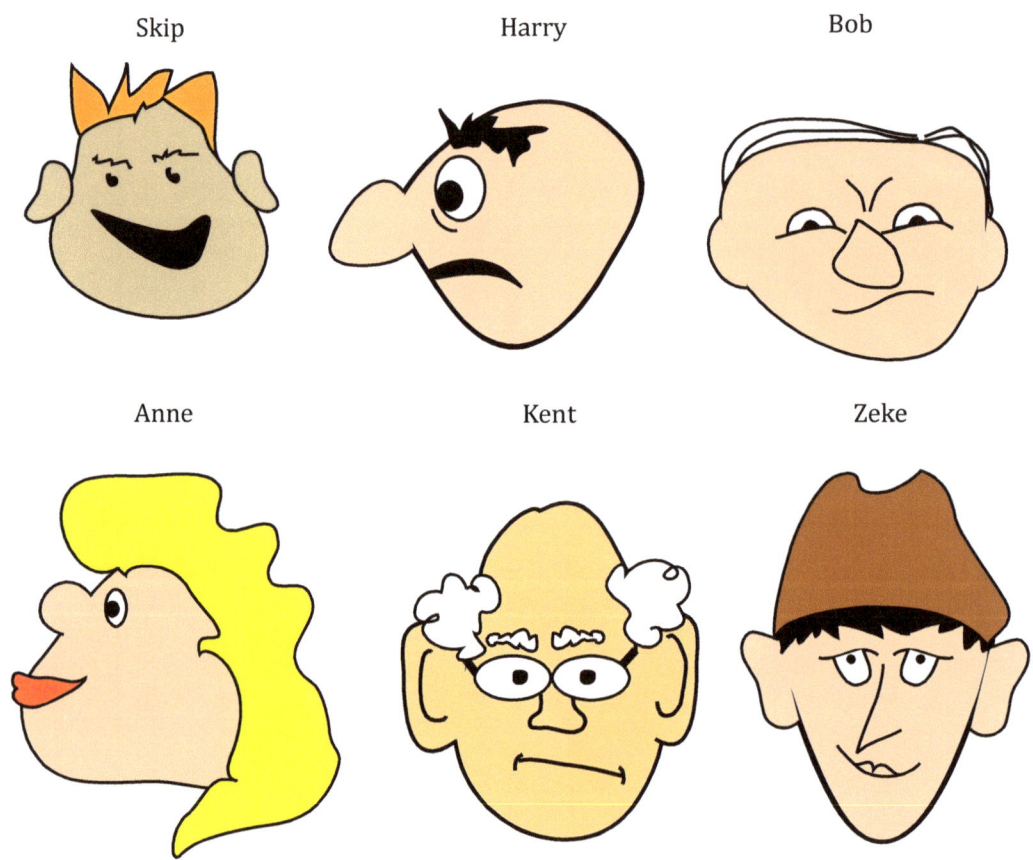

Skip

Harry

Bob

Anne

Kent

Zeke

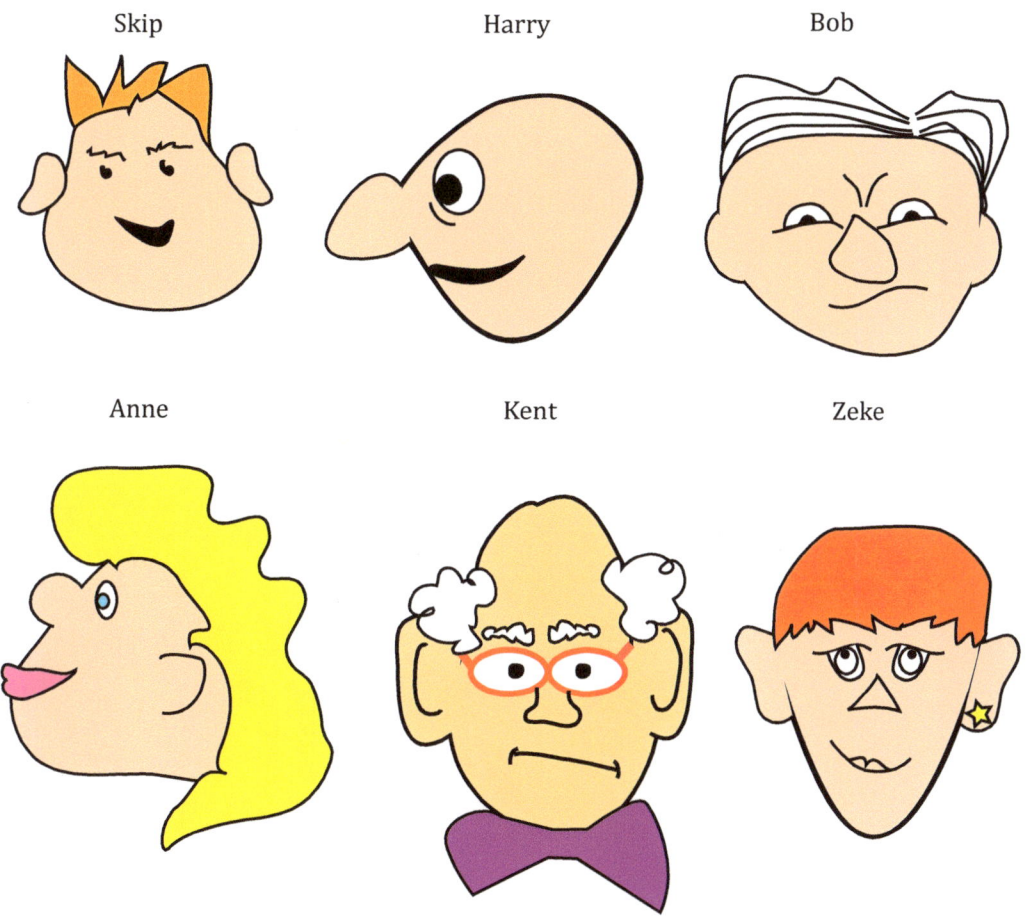

There are 23 things that have been changed in the bottom picture. You'll probably notice some of them right away but others are more subtle. Don't forget to look at colors. If a color is lighter or darker or if it's just a different color, then it counts as a difference. There are a lot of differences, so make a list on a separate sheet.

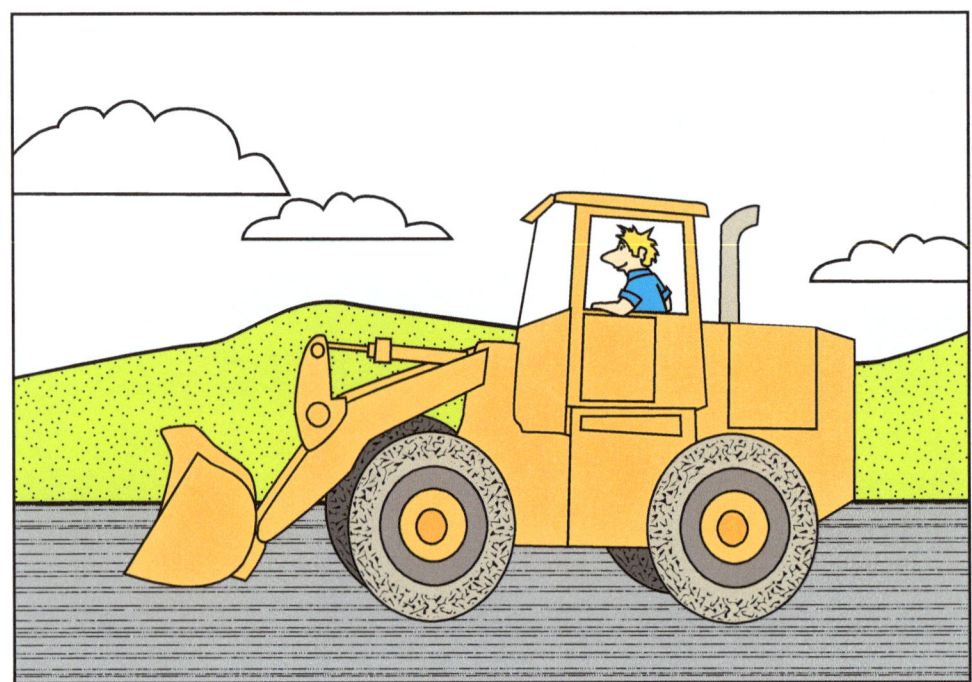

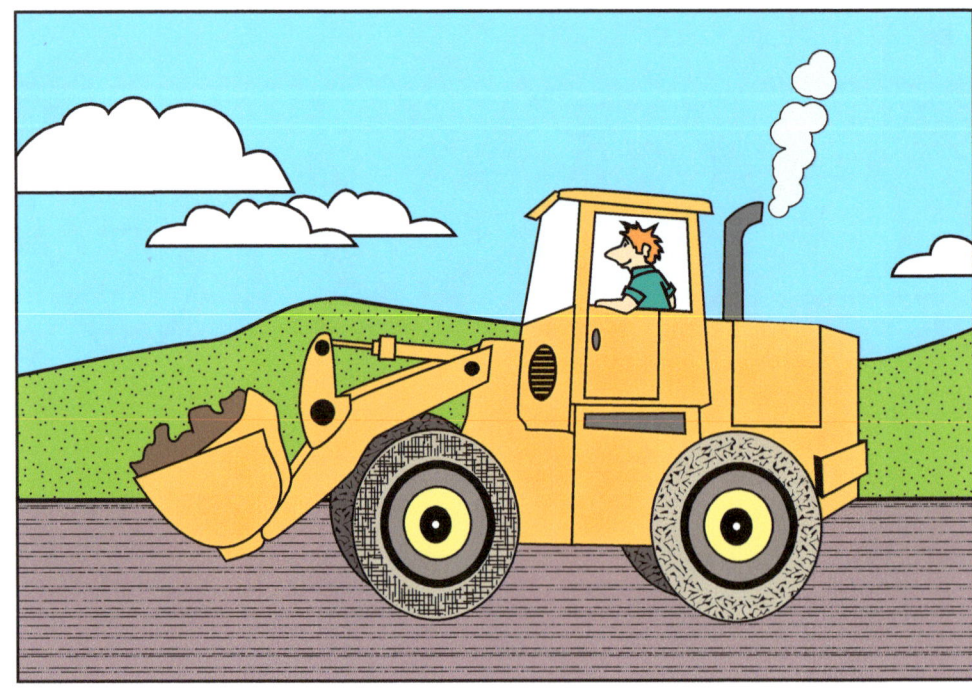

Here is Ronnie again. There are eight differences in the bottom rooster. See if you can find all eight. The grid lines are there to help you notice and compare things. Some parts haven't changed in shape but the shape has been shifted to a new location. If the lines of the drawing don't fit the boxes of the grid exactly the same way, that's your clue that you've found a difference. Look closely to see what has actually changed.

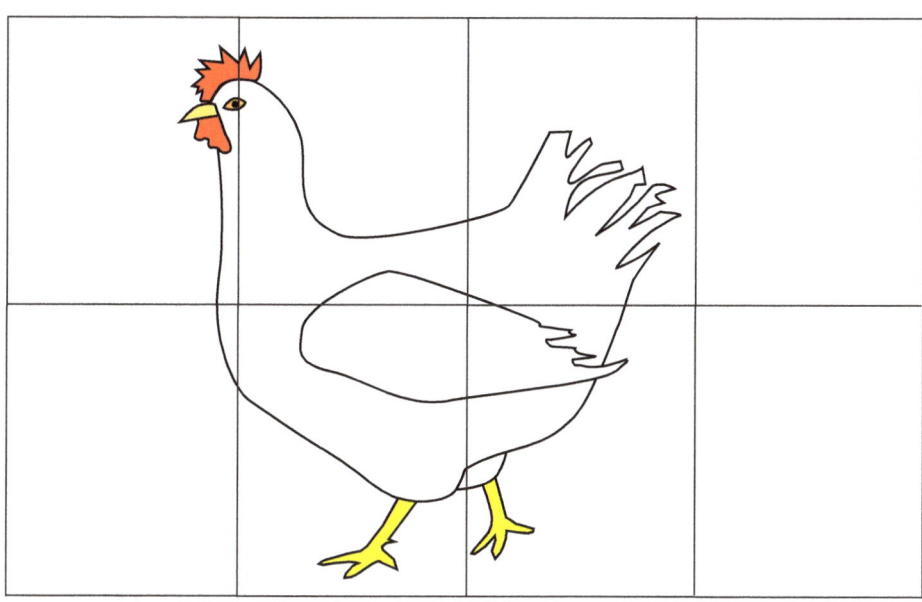

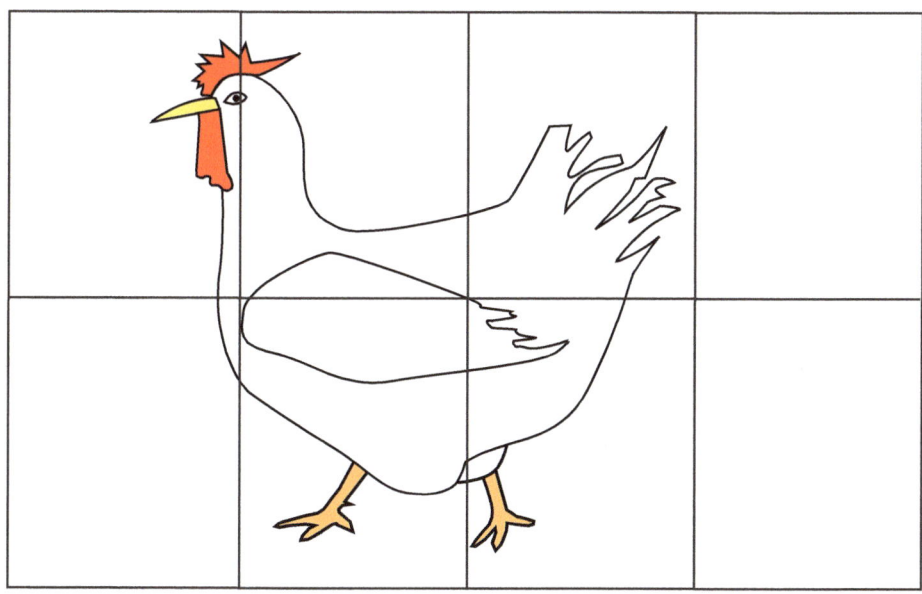

Draw this dog in the bottom grid exactly as you see it in the top grid. Make sure your lines fit the boxes in precisely the same way, paying attention to how close lines are to edges or where lines cross the grid. When you're done, go back and compare each of the eight boxes in the grid separately to see how well it matches and make any corrections to your drawing. Use pencil rather than pen so you can erase if necessary.

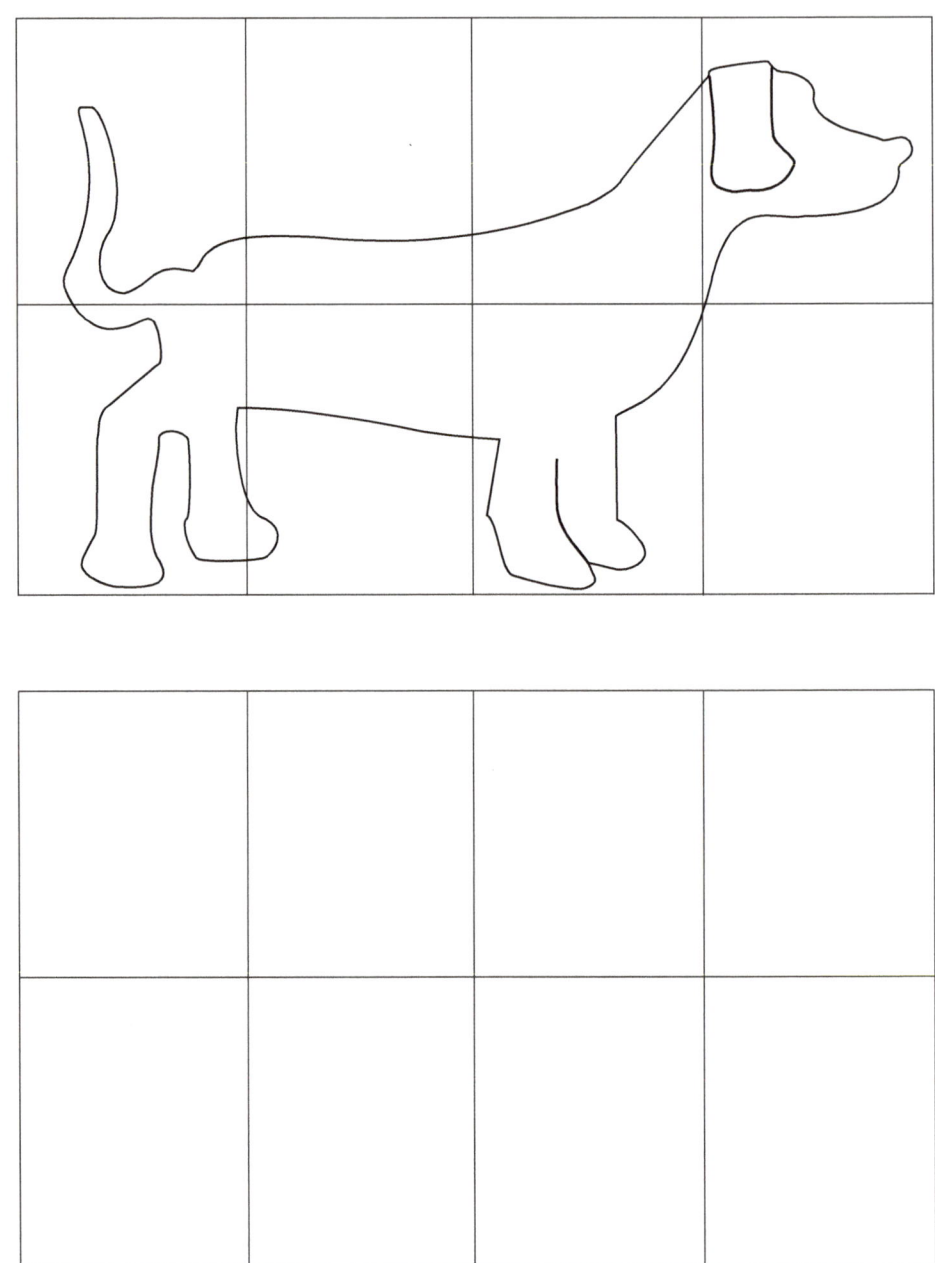

There are twelve things that are different in the bottom picture. Take your time or you'll miss some. If you're having trouble finding all twelve, compare each of the eight boxes in the grid individually. If the lines don't fit the box in exactly the same way, that tells you there's a difference there but you'll need to discover what it is. Either write the list of differences in your book or on a separate sheet of paper.

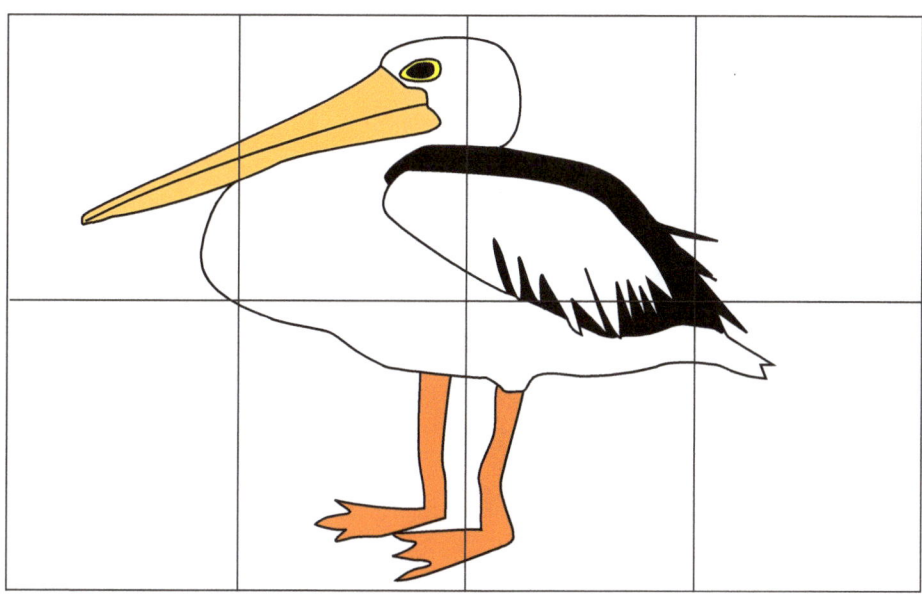

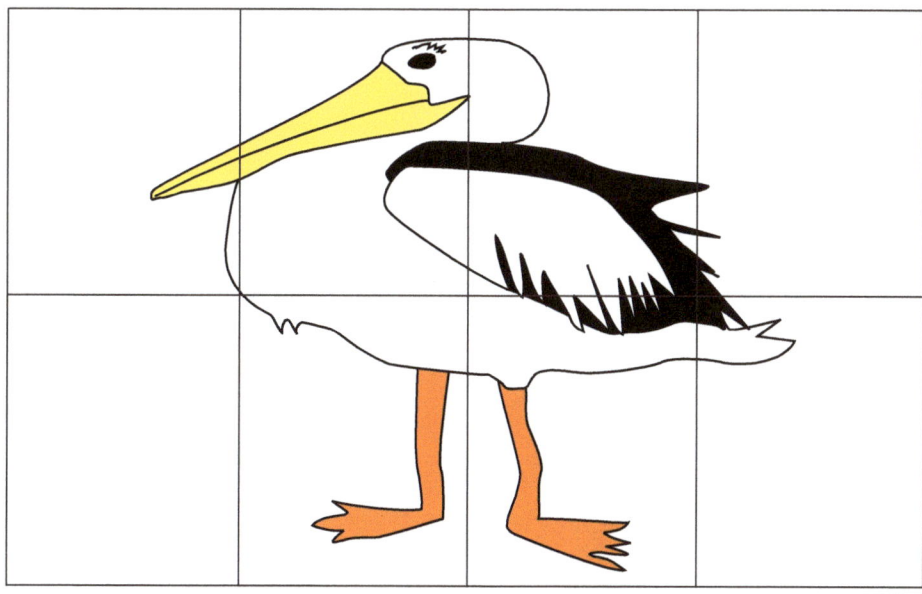

There are eleven things that have been changed in *picture 2*. Compare the pictures until you can find all eleven. Some are easy to see but others are more subtle. Don't hurry. Put a small X on each difference to keep track or, if you prefer, write them down on separate sheet of paper. Resist looking up the answer until you've found all eleven differences.

picture 1

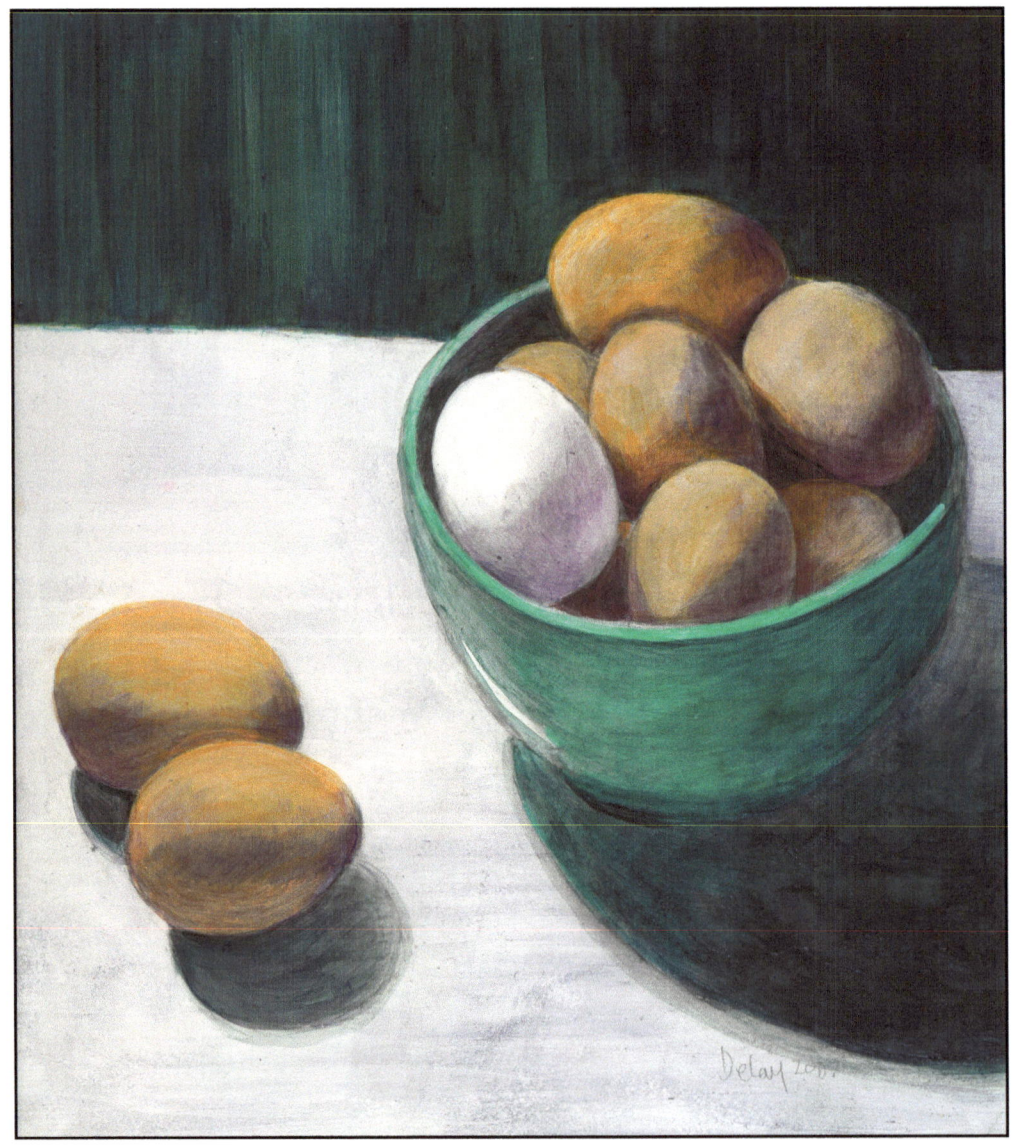

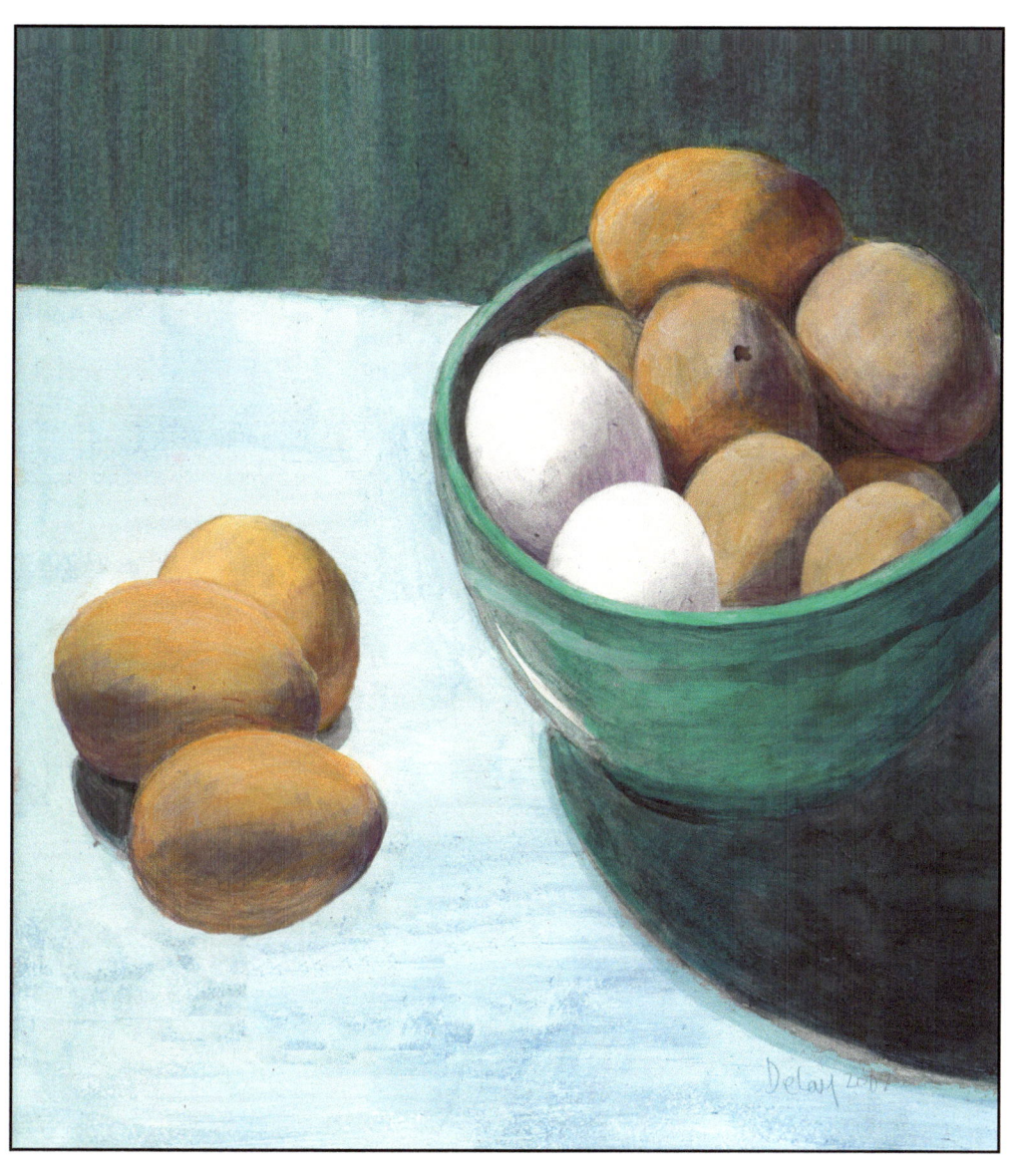

First look at the boxed apple and jar on the left. Notice the space between the pair. There are six other pairs but only two of them are the same distance apart as those in the box. Can you find the two pairs that match?

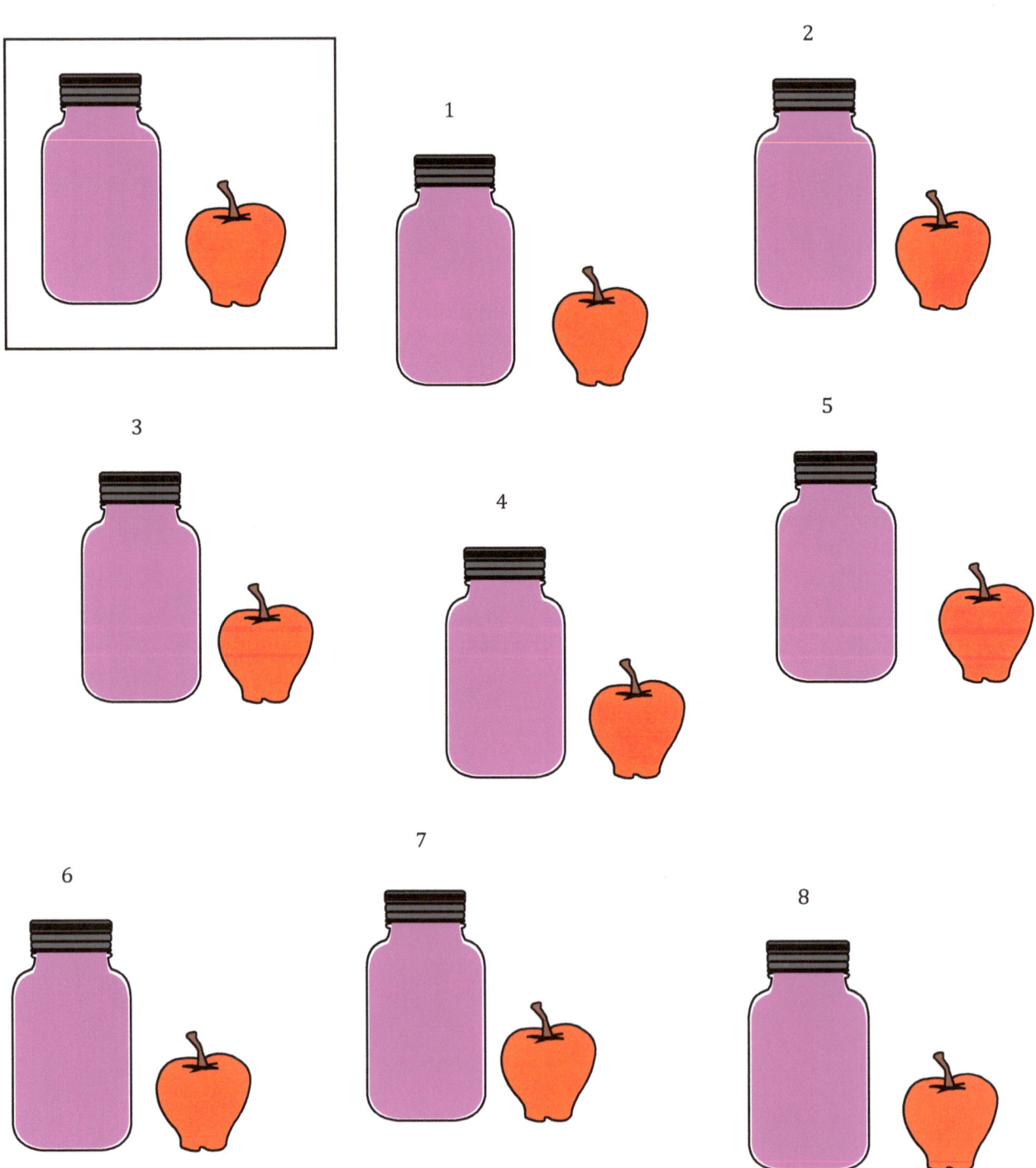

Matching Angles

Medium

Two of the 14 lines below are slanted at different angles than the rest. Which two are different?

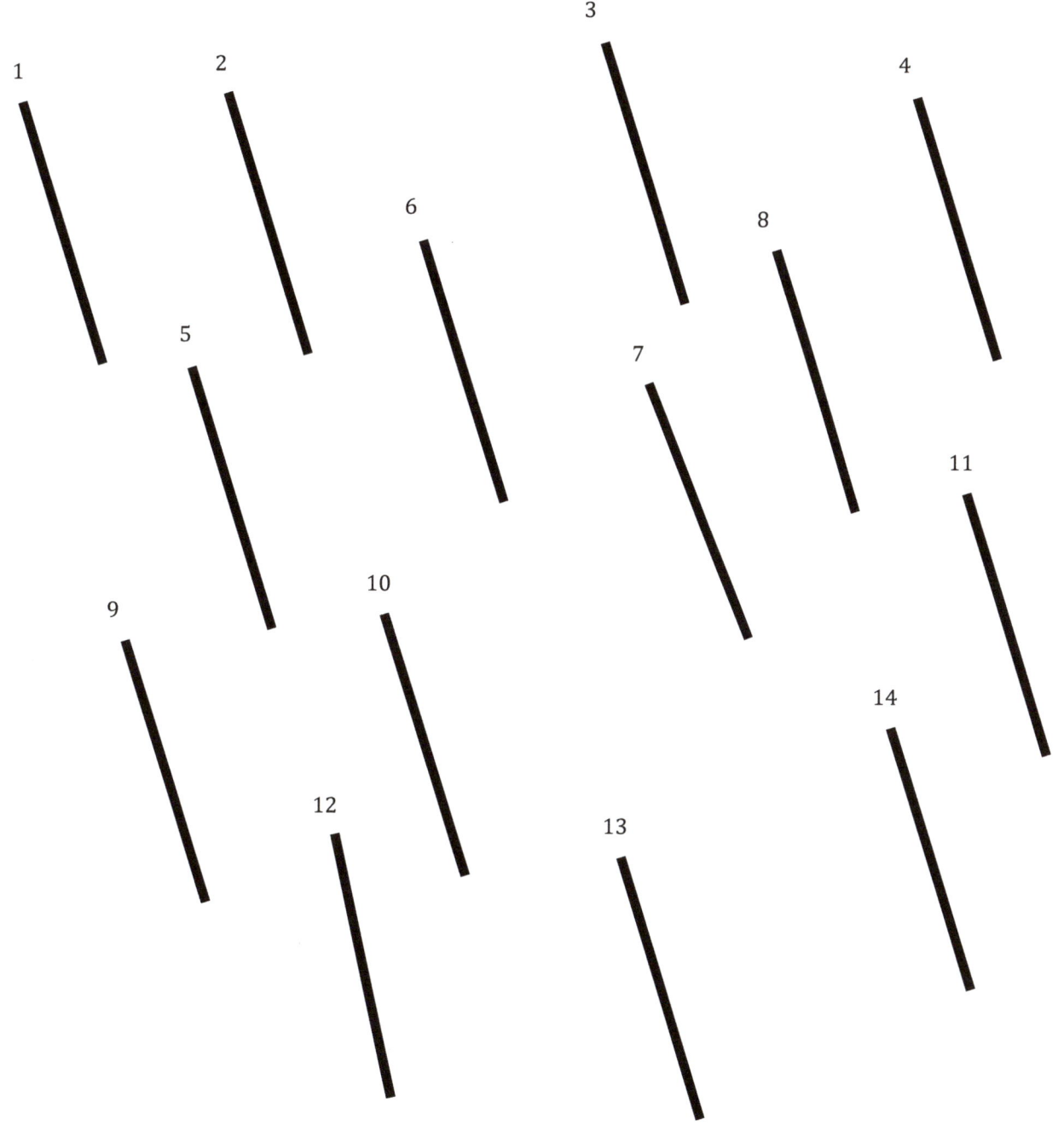

Using a pencil, draw the outline of the rabbit in the bottom grid exactly as it is in the top. Pay attention to how the lines fit into the individual boxes and make your lines fit in the same way. Avoid thinking about drawing a rabbit. Your task will seem easier if you concentrate on just drawing a set of lines that need to fit precisely into a gridded box.

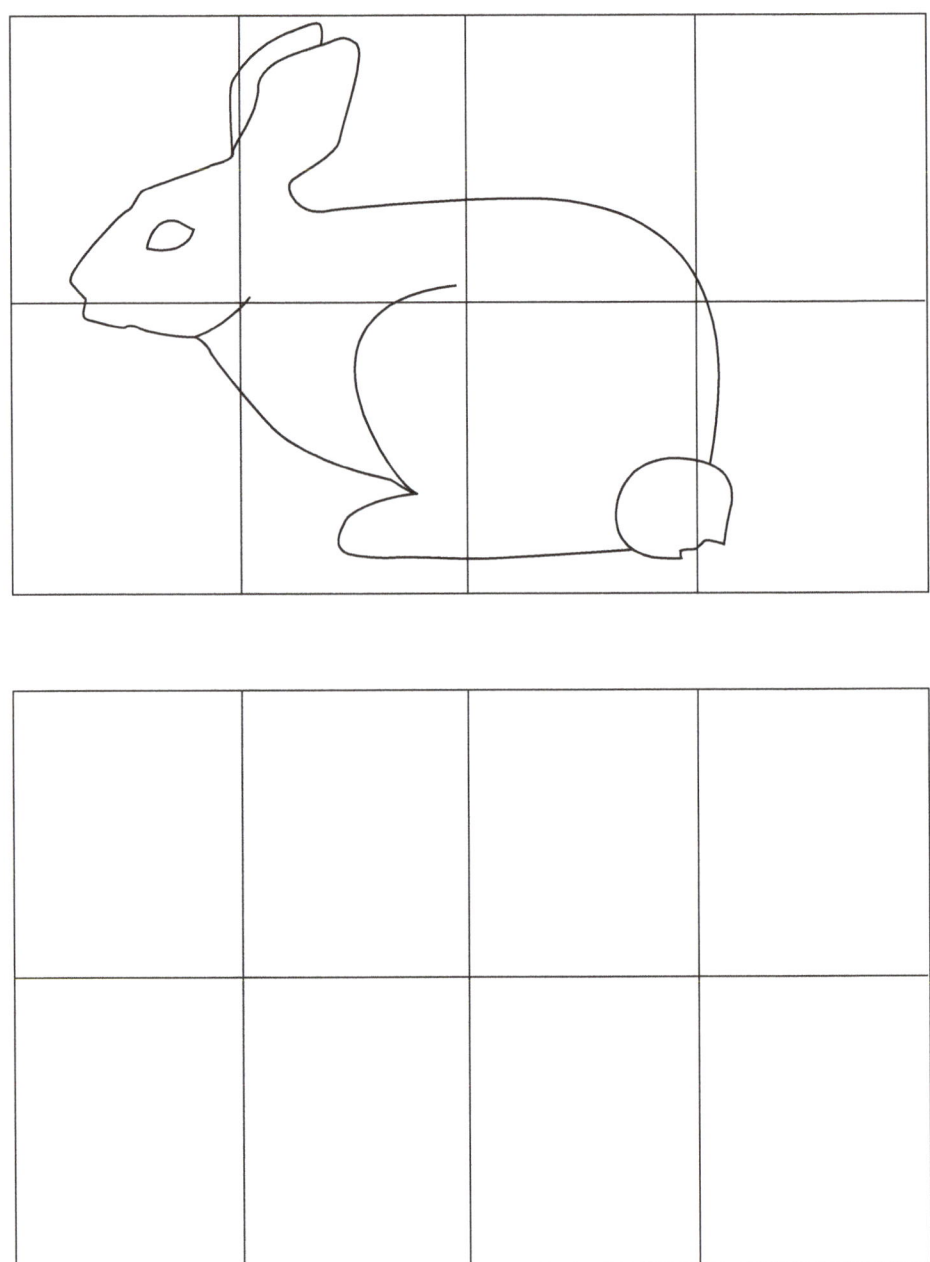

Find the 14 changes made to the bottom group of vegetables. It will make it easier to keep track of them if you write a list on a separate sheet of paper. Don't forget to pay attention to differences in color or shade of color. Some of the vegetables were moved from one place to another but that only counts as one difference.

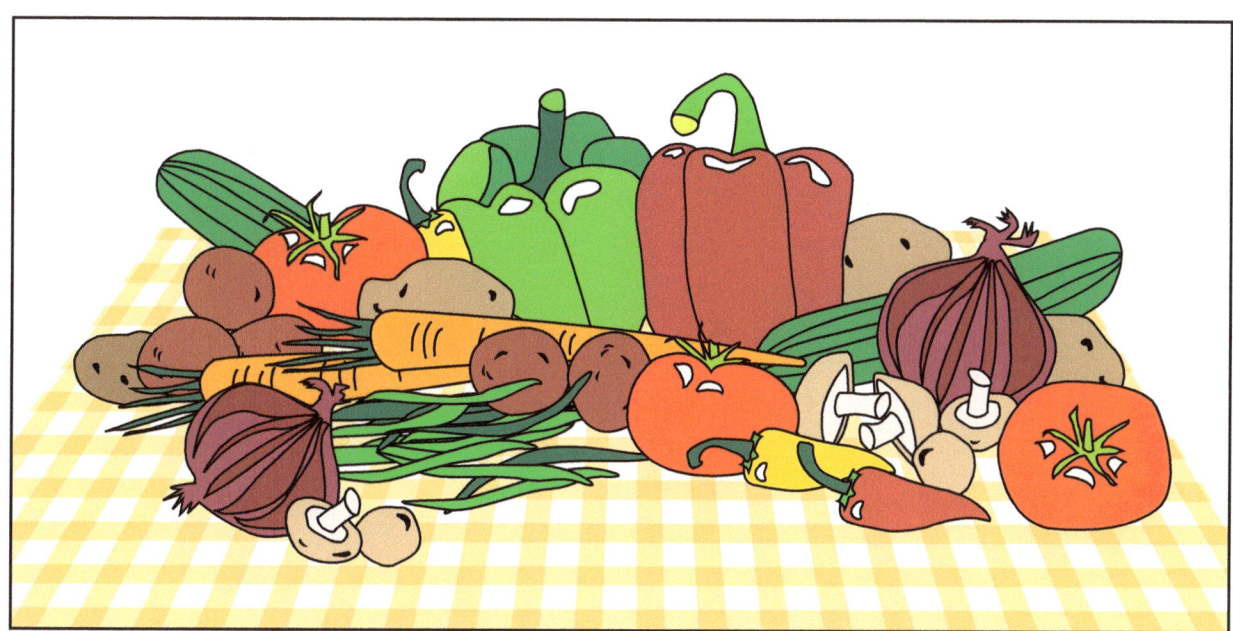

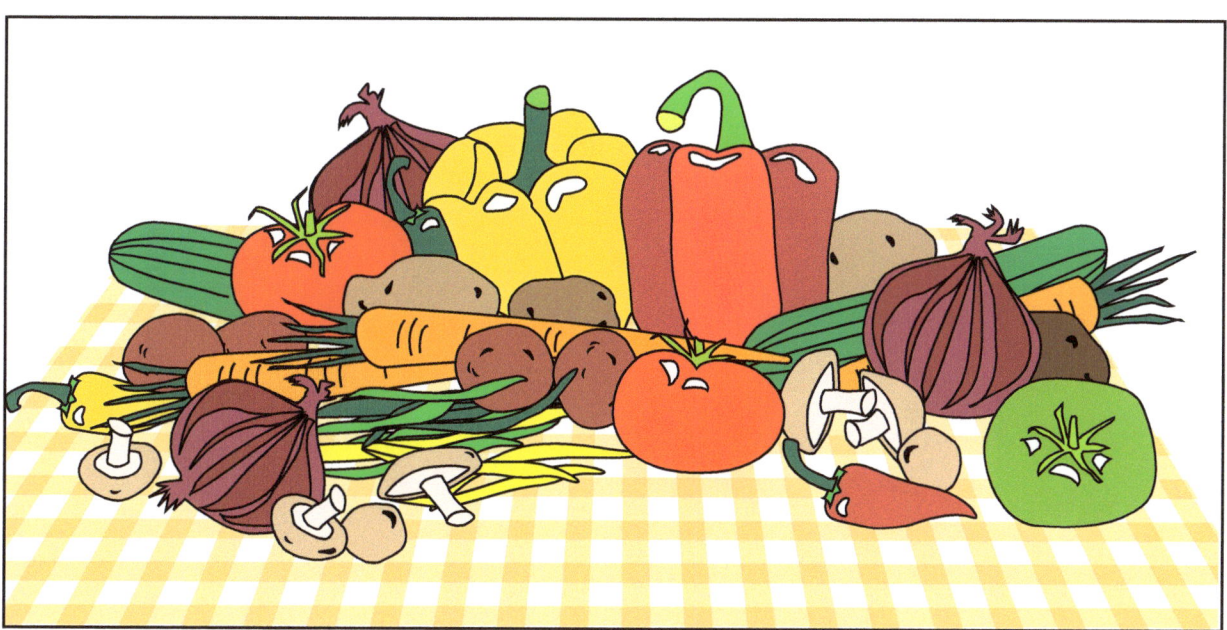

The gazelle herd is made up of four types of gazelles that are very similar but not the same. Take a good look at Greta. There are six gazelles that look exactly like her in the herd. Which ones are just like Greta? Remember that there are three other styles of gazelle so look for their differences. Don't worry about size. Size is not considered a difference here.

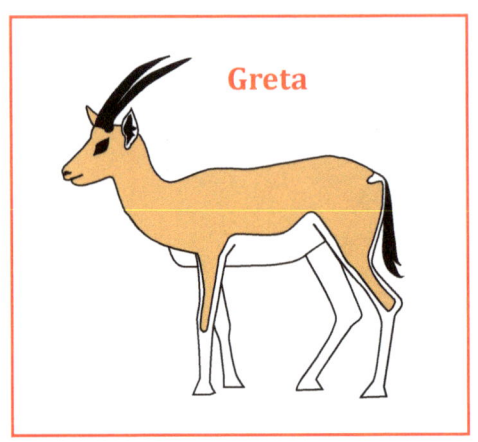

Greta

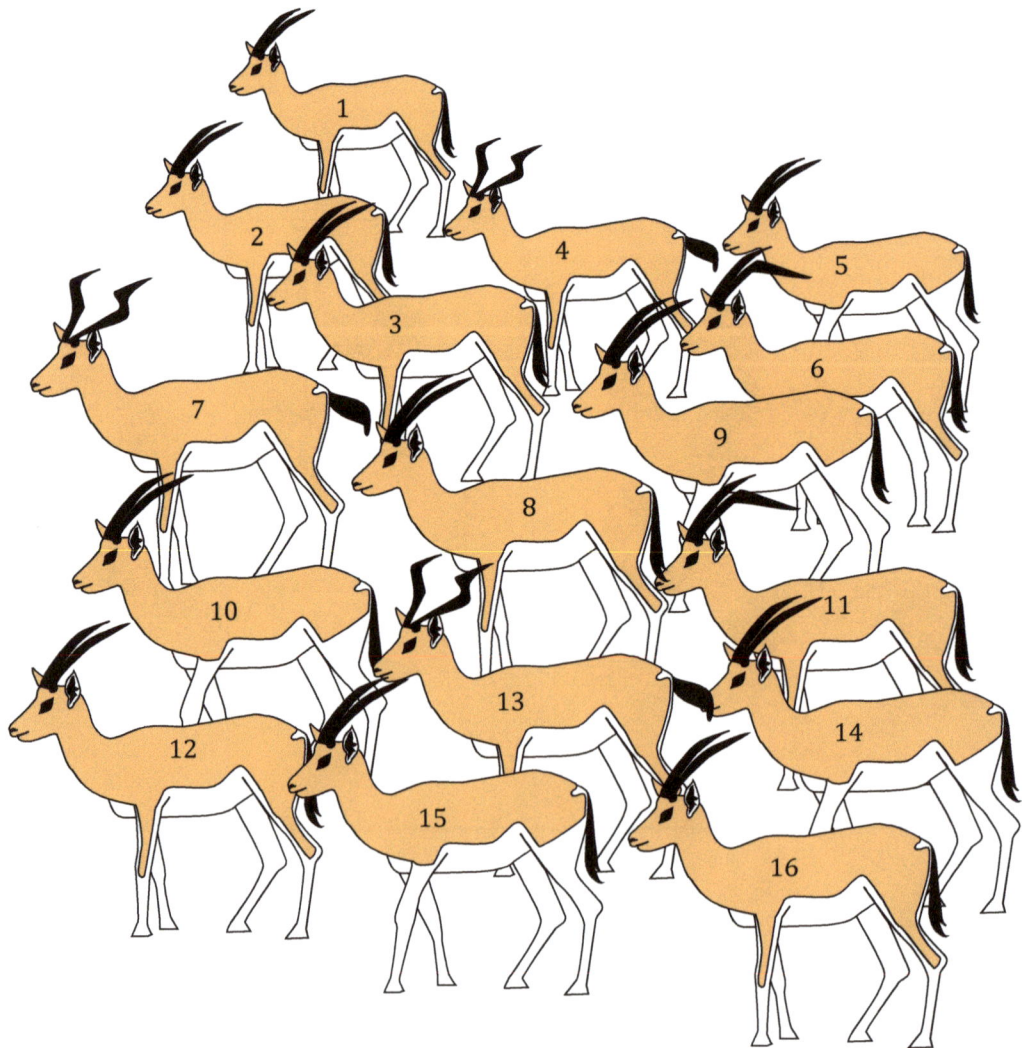

Matching Angles

Medium

Look at the giraffe in the red box. The angle of the slant of his neck is what you should pay attention to. One other giraffe's neck matches that angle. Which one matches?

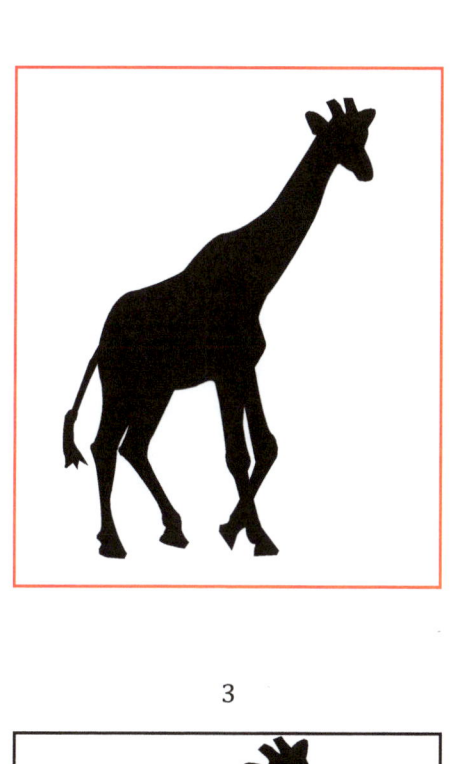

1

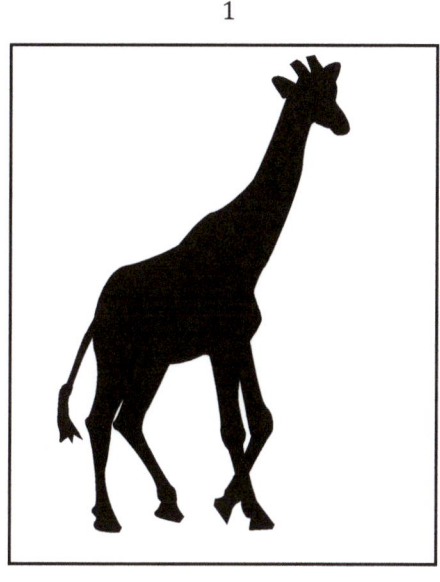

2

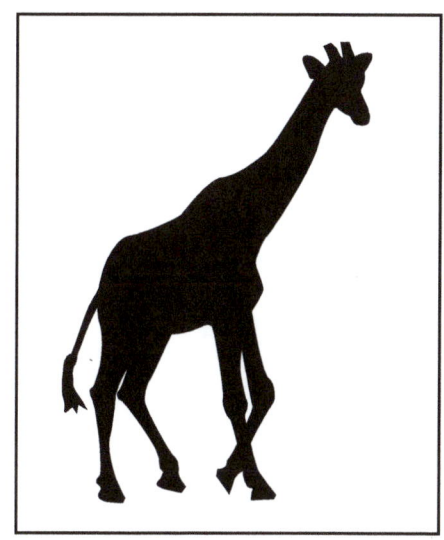

3

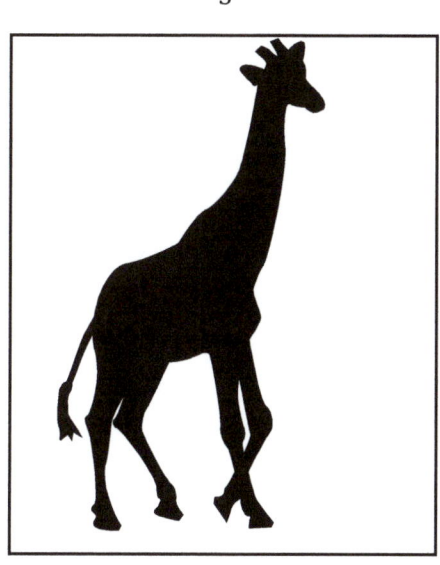

4

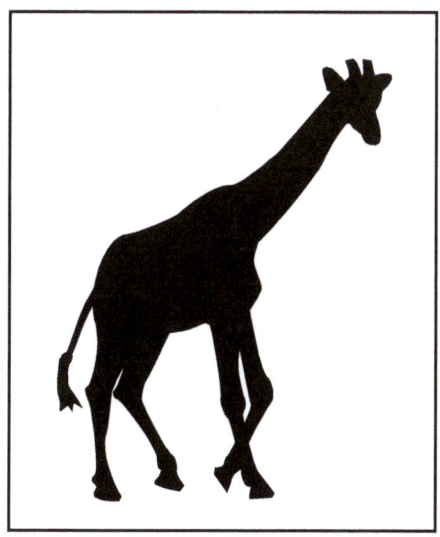

5

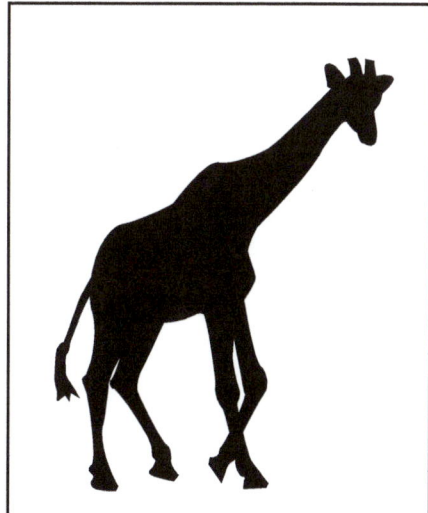

Ten things are different in *photo 2*. Look back and forth between the two until you can find all ten. Some are easier to catch than others so don't hurry. In order for your artist eye to be trained, you must slow down.

photo 1

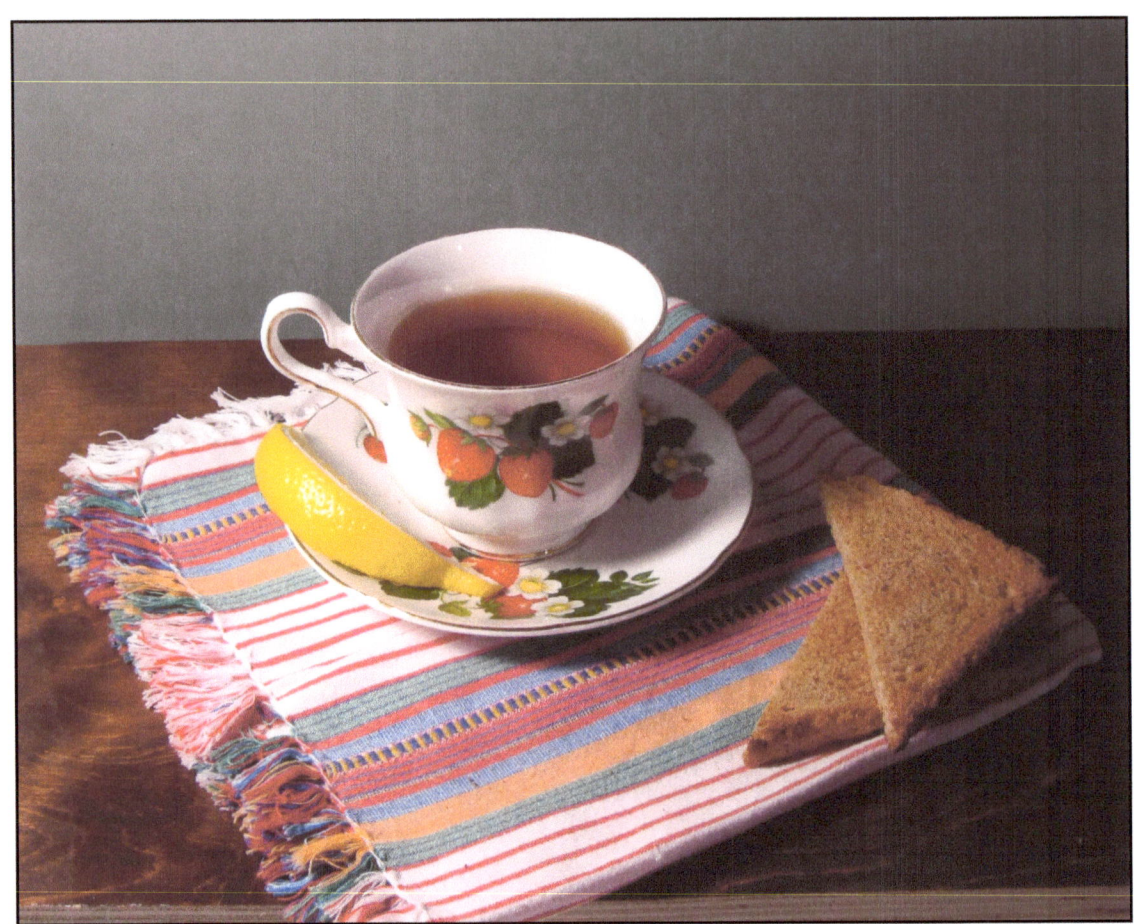

photo 2

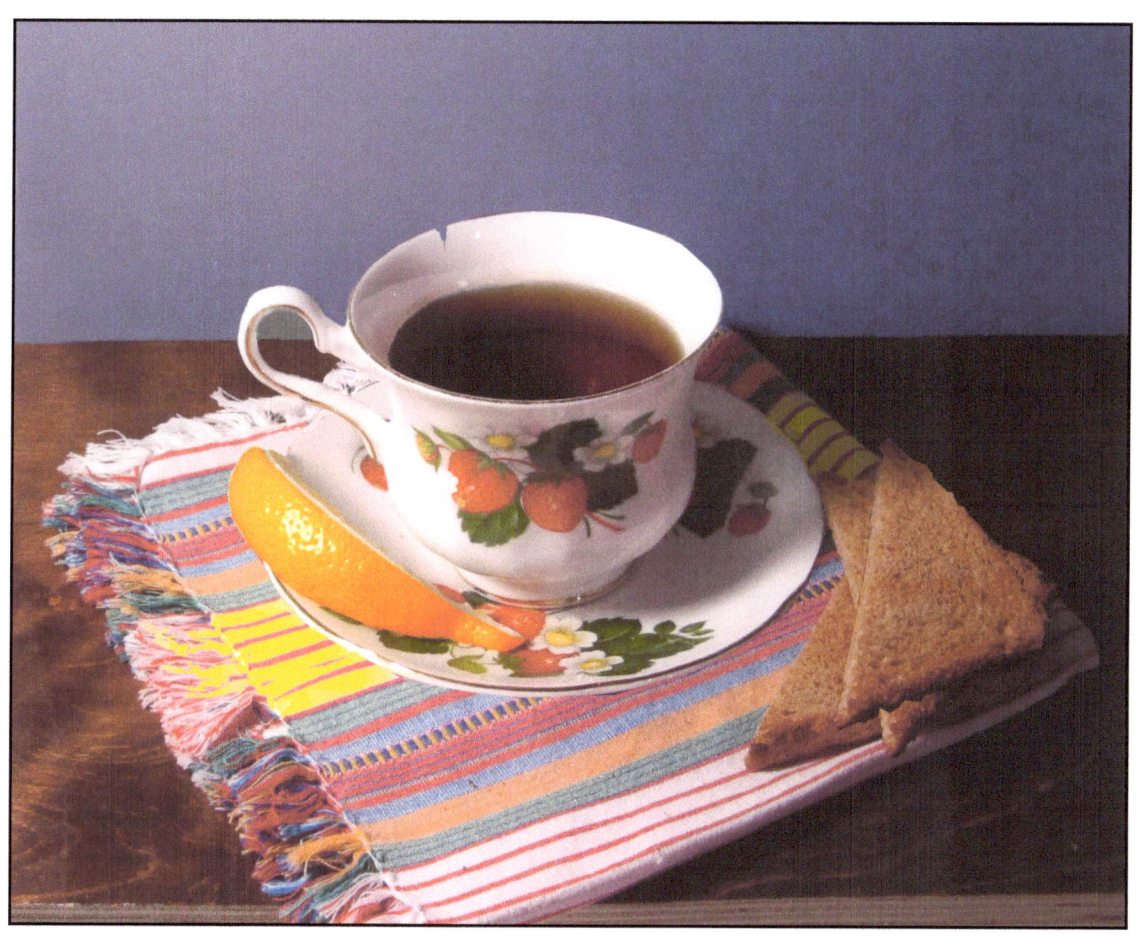

You will be completing these drawings of symmetrical vases (the same on both sides.) Draw in the right side on each so it's a mirror image of the left side like you flipped it over. Pay careful attention to how the curves fit in the boxes on the left side and use that as a guide for how you draw the right side. How close do the curved lines come to the outer edge? Where do the curves cross the lines of the grid? Go slowly so you can scan back and forth as you draw. Use a pencil so you can erase. When you finish, go back and check each box to see if the lines fit the same way. Make corrections if you need to.

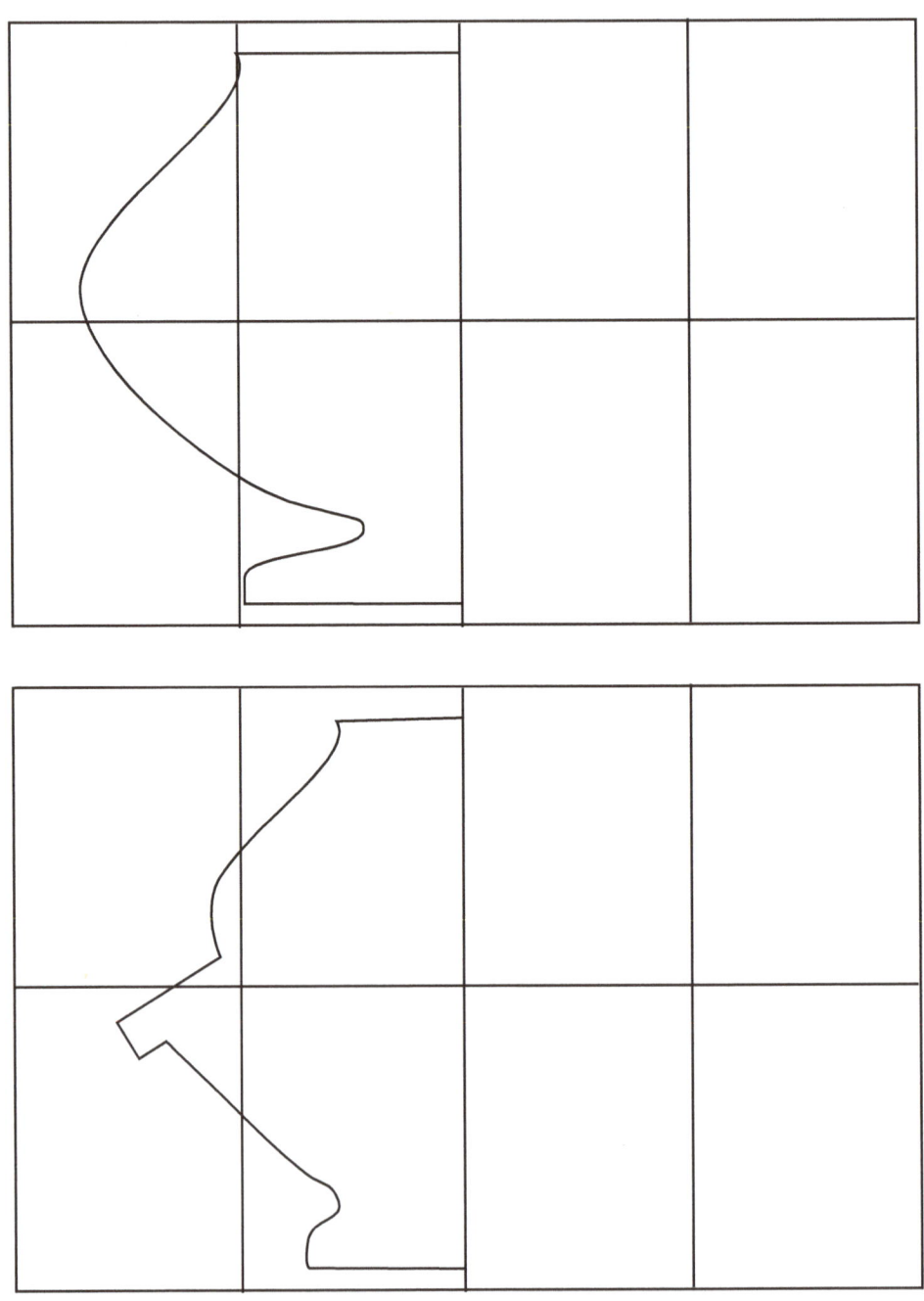

Only one of the 12 numbered butterflies has the same markings as the one in the red box? Which is it?

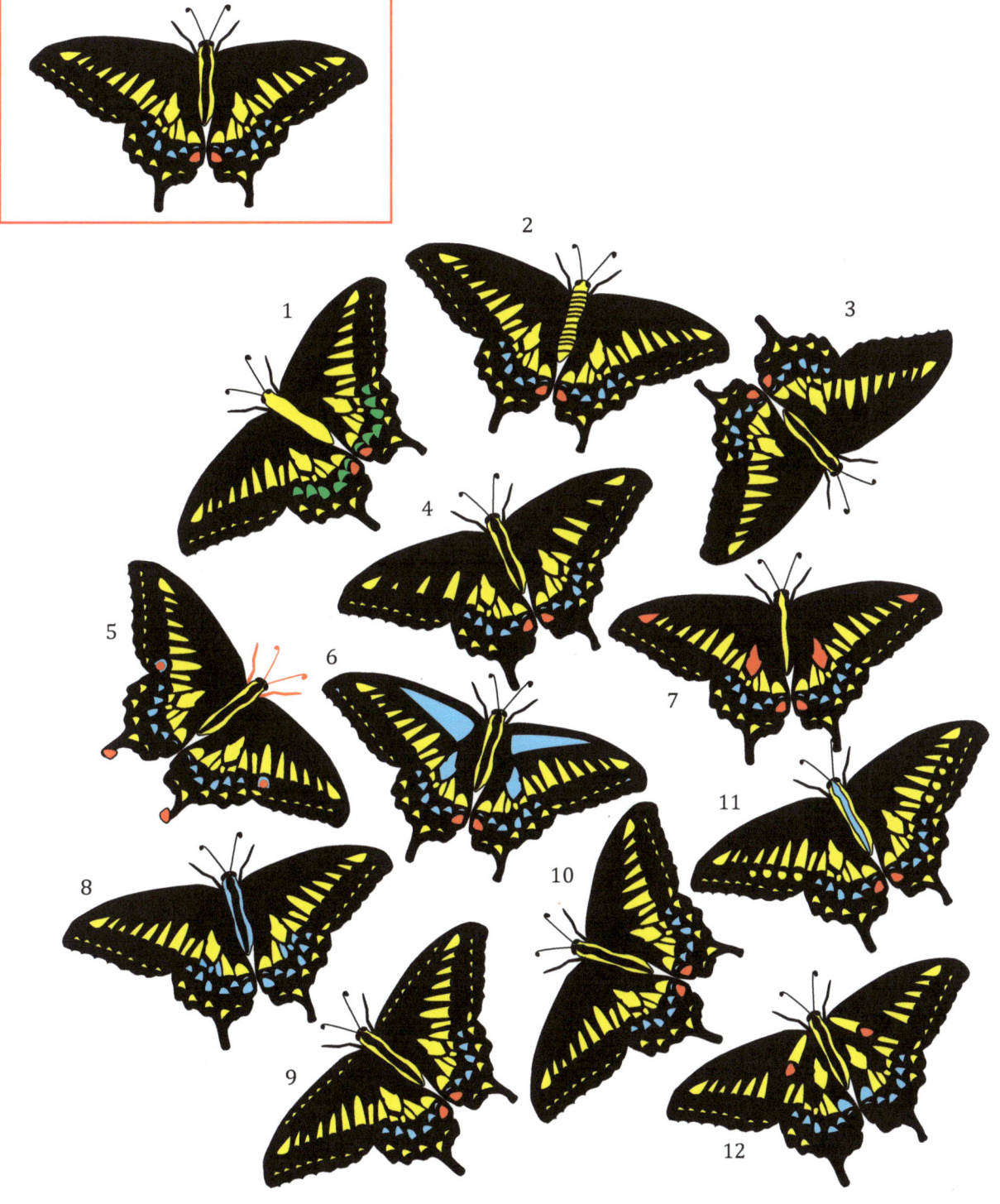

Look carefully at the black spots on the cow in the photo. Using a pencil, lightly draw the shapes of the spots and their exact placement into the line drawing below. None of the spots is round so don't get lazy and just draw dots. Pay attention to how close a spot is to the edge of the cow or to another spot. When you think you have the shapes and placement right, color in the spots with a black marker or your pencil.

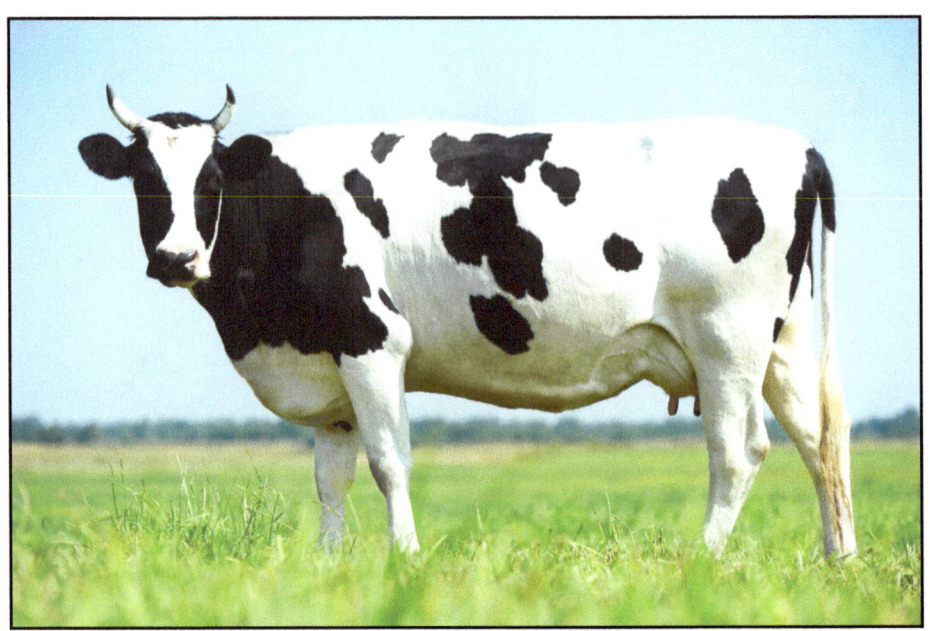

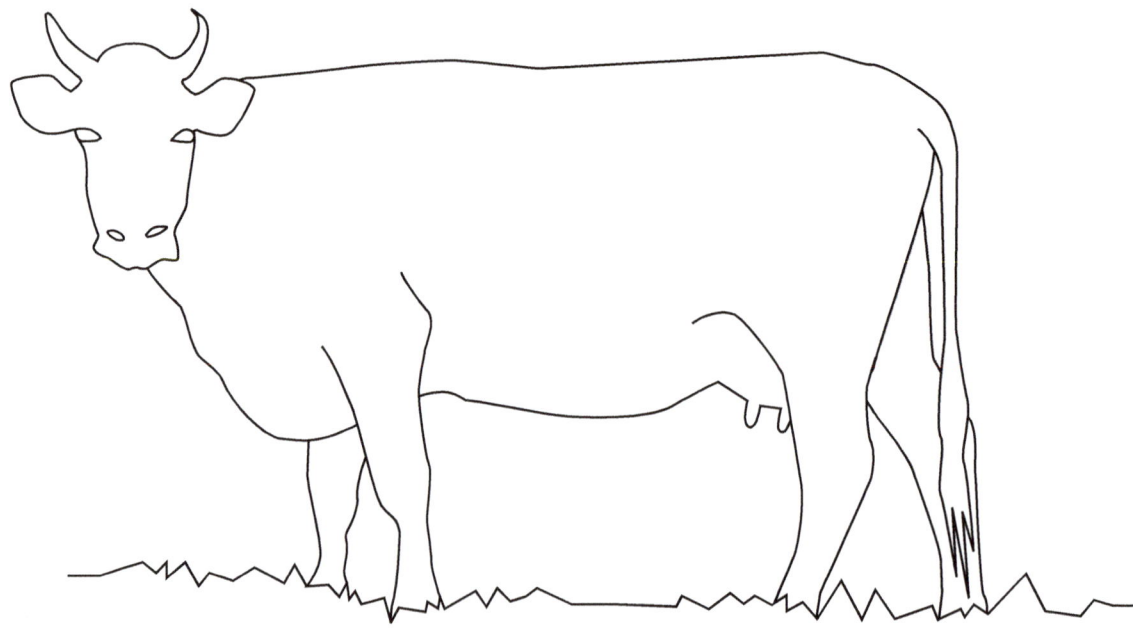

Draw It

You've studied the cow and where the spots go, now it's time to draw the cow. Using a pencil, lightly draw in the outline of the cow so that it fits the bottom grid exactly like you see in the top grid. When you're satisfied with your outline, add the spots in again and color them in with your pencil.

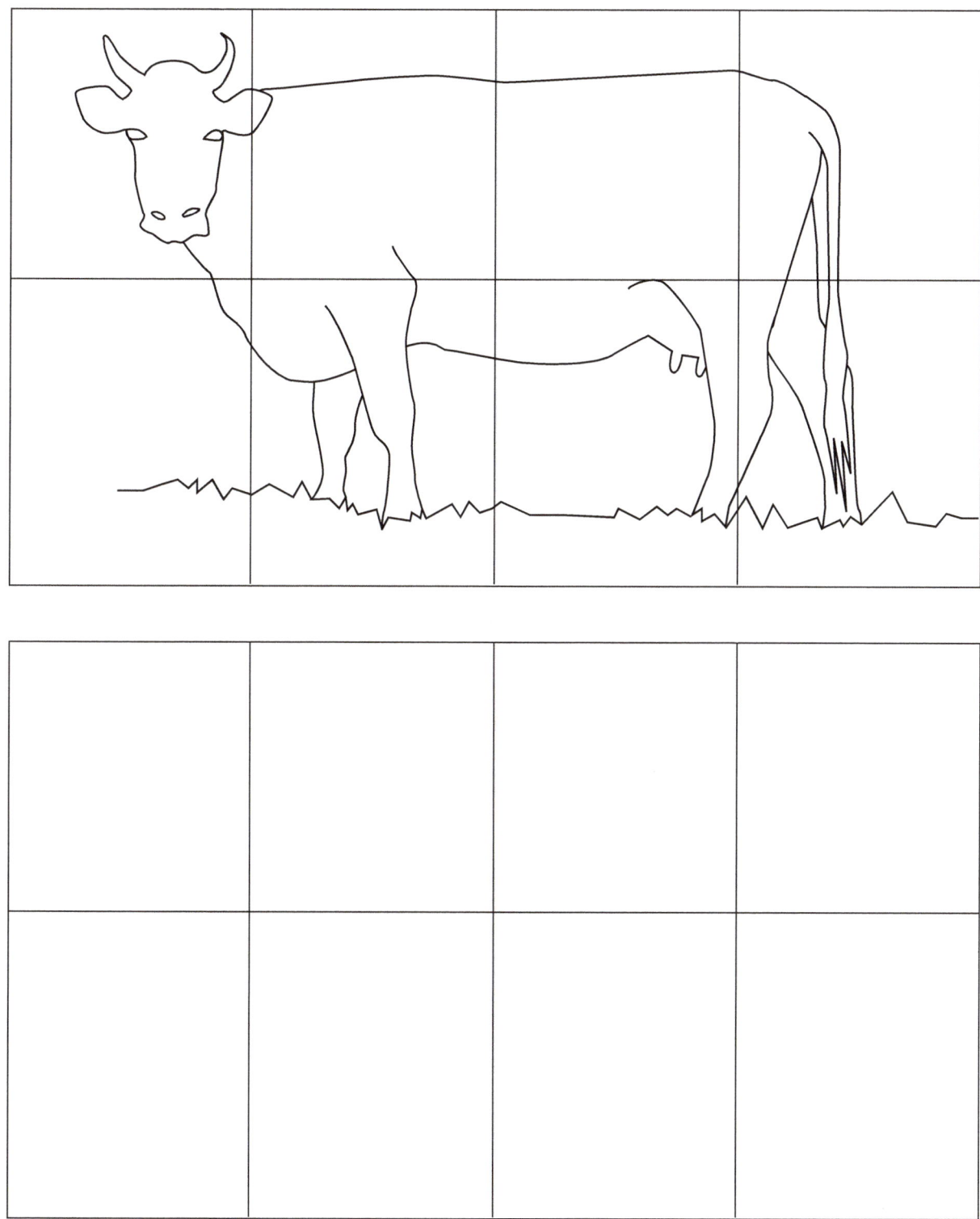

Sometimes it's really hard to tell one color from another that's similar. Our perception of a color is influenced by the colors that surround it, so if we put that color on a different color background, it looks like a different color. The good news is that with practice we can get much better at perceiving color differences.

The shapes of the flower parts on the following page are the same ones used in the collage below, but some of the colors have been altered. There are seven that are identical. Some of the pieces have been rotated to fit on the page so don't let that confuse you. Shape and color are the only important things in this exercise. See if you can pick out the pieces that are exactly the same color and shape as those used in the collage.

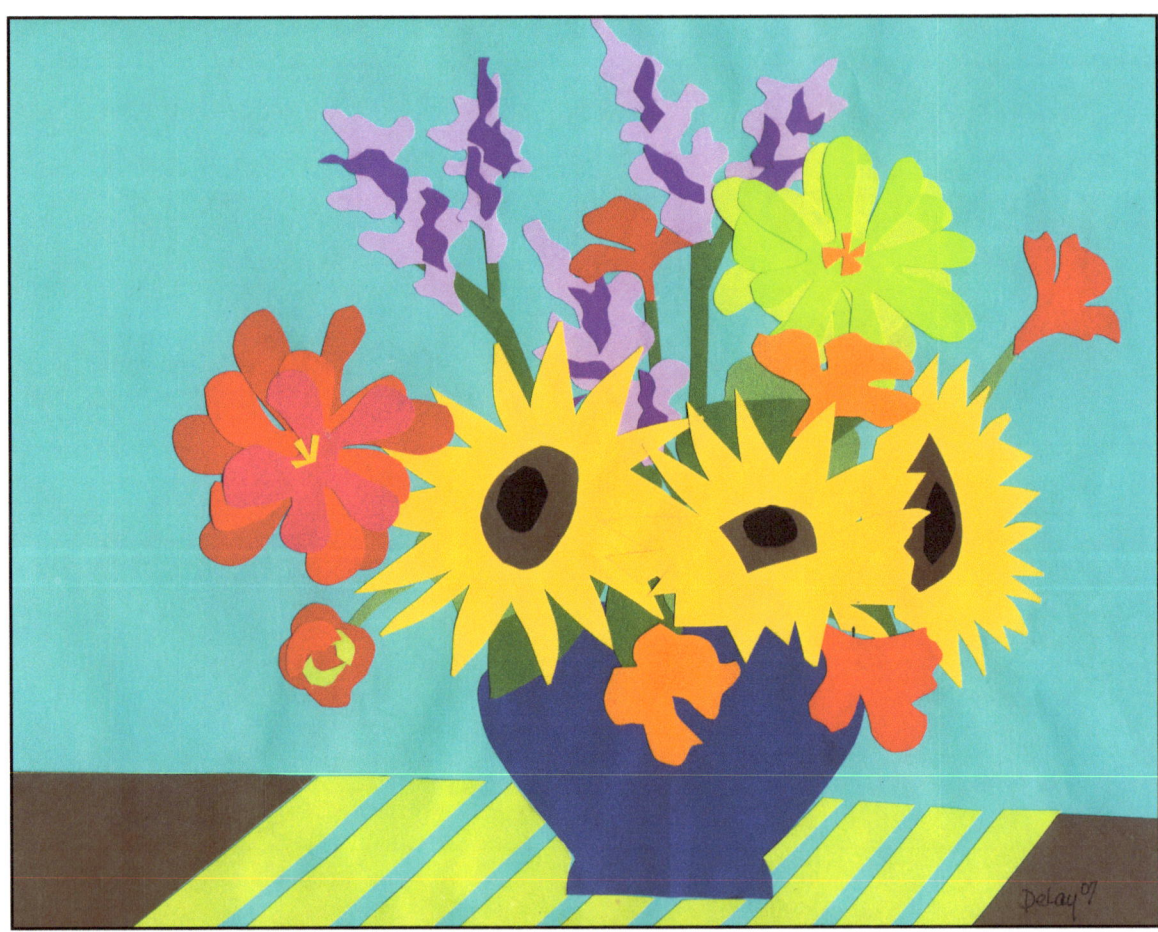

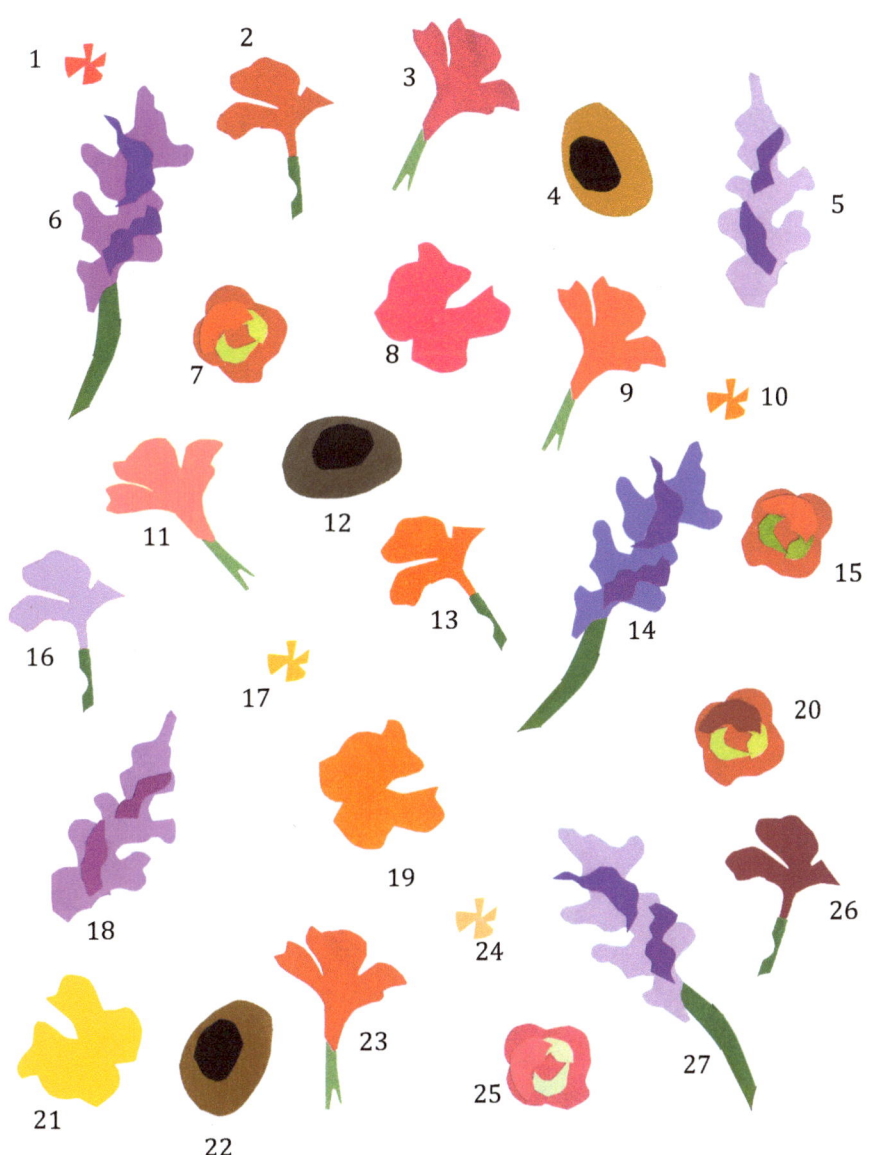

1
2
3
4
5
6
7
8
9
10
11
12
13
14
15
16
17
18
19
20
21
22
23
24
25
26
27

Carefully compare *photo 1* with *photo 2*. There are twelve things that are different in *photo 2*. The differences are not obvious so don't get discouraged if you don't see them right away. Take your time and study the two photos. Try looking at one thing in the picture at a time and comparing just that one thing in the two photos.

photo 1

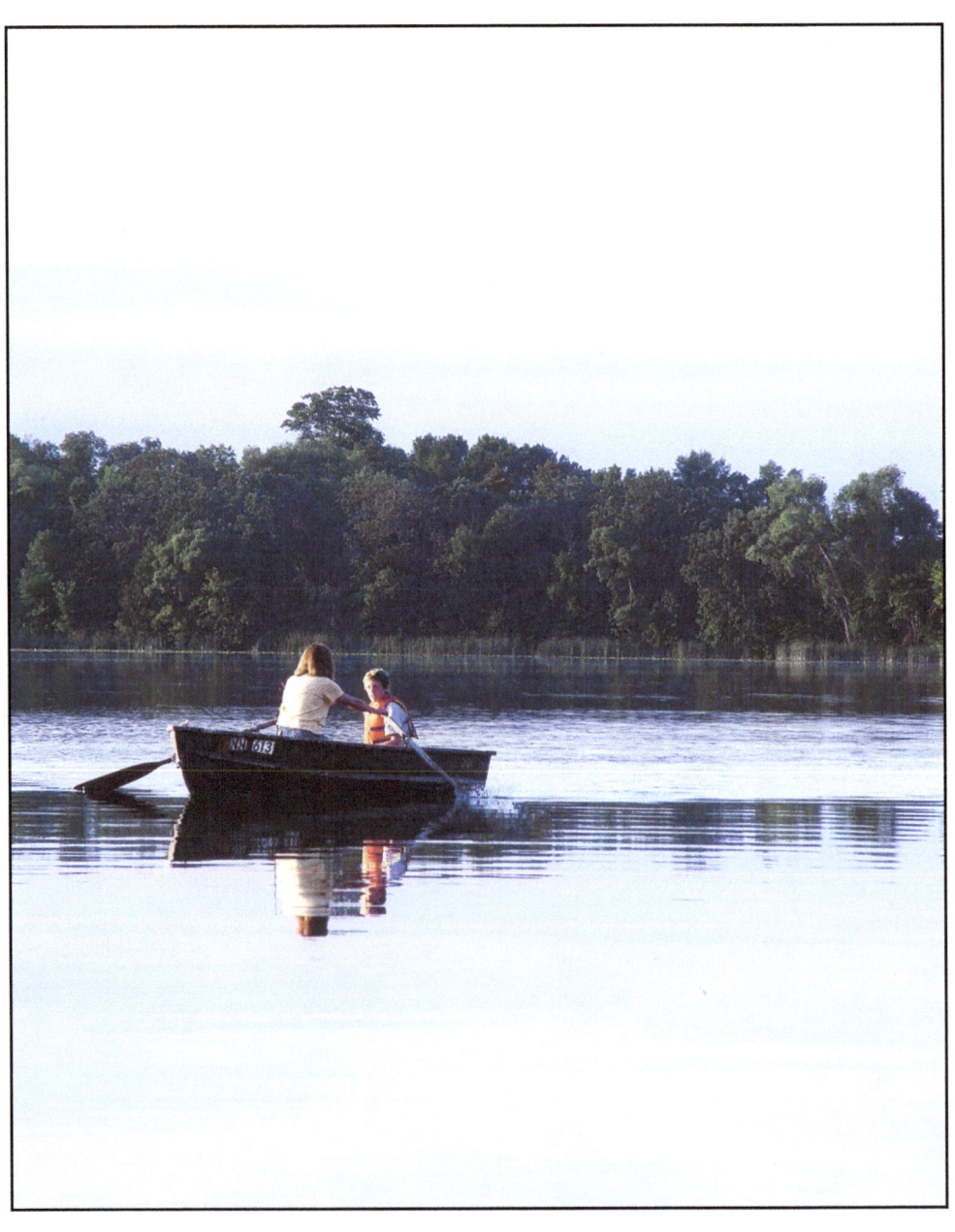

photo 2

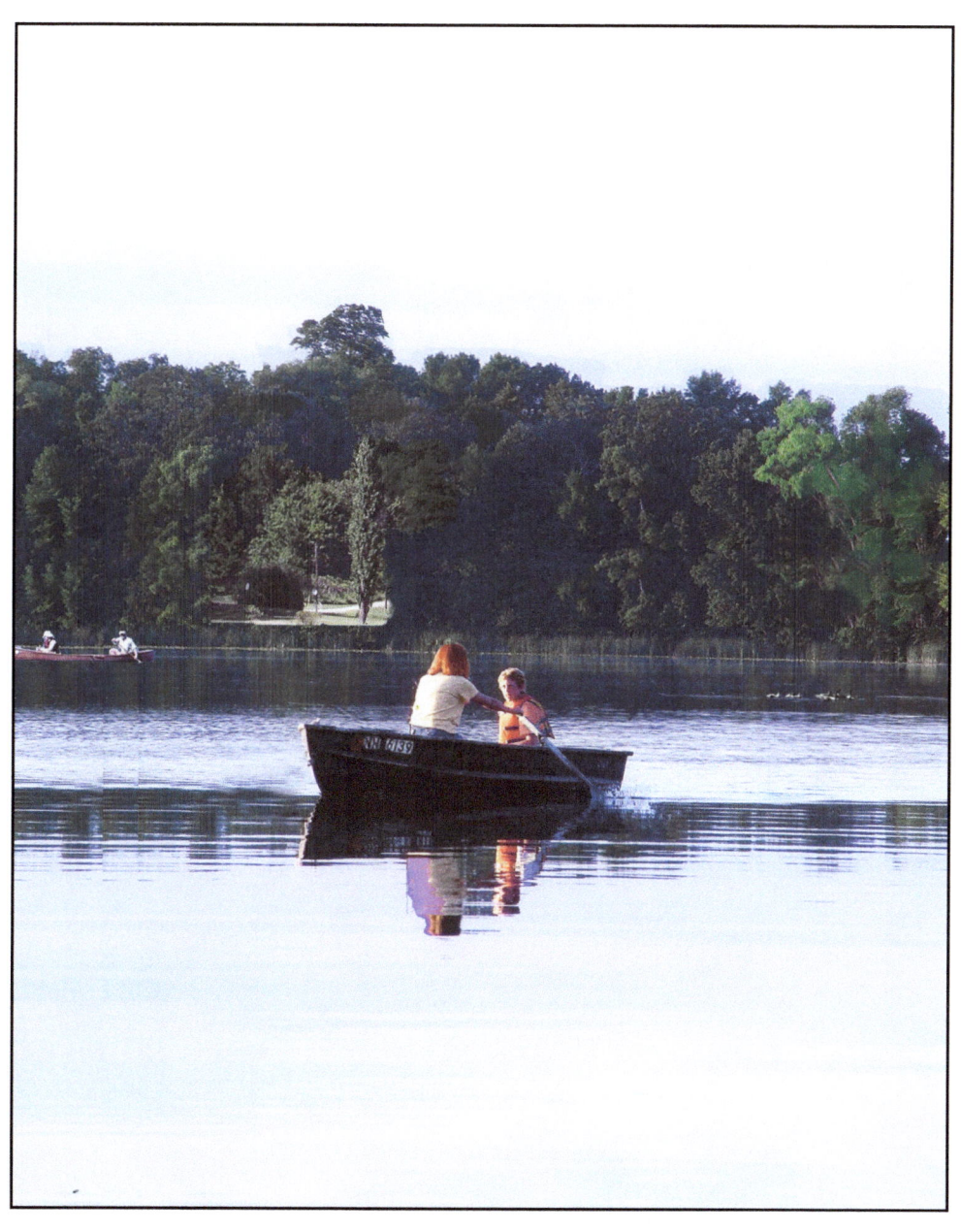

One of the six line drawings on the following page was traced over this photo of a farm so it matches exactly. The others were changed and don't match. There is only one thing that's different in each of the five wrong drawings but the difference is not obvious so take your time and study the drawings. Which one matches?

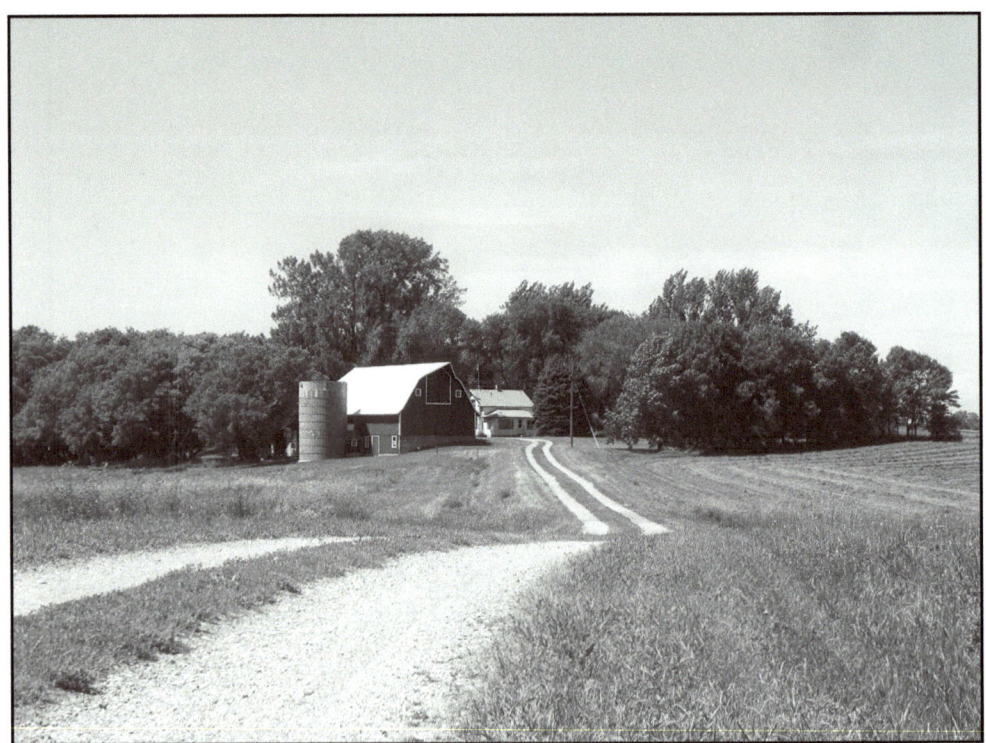

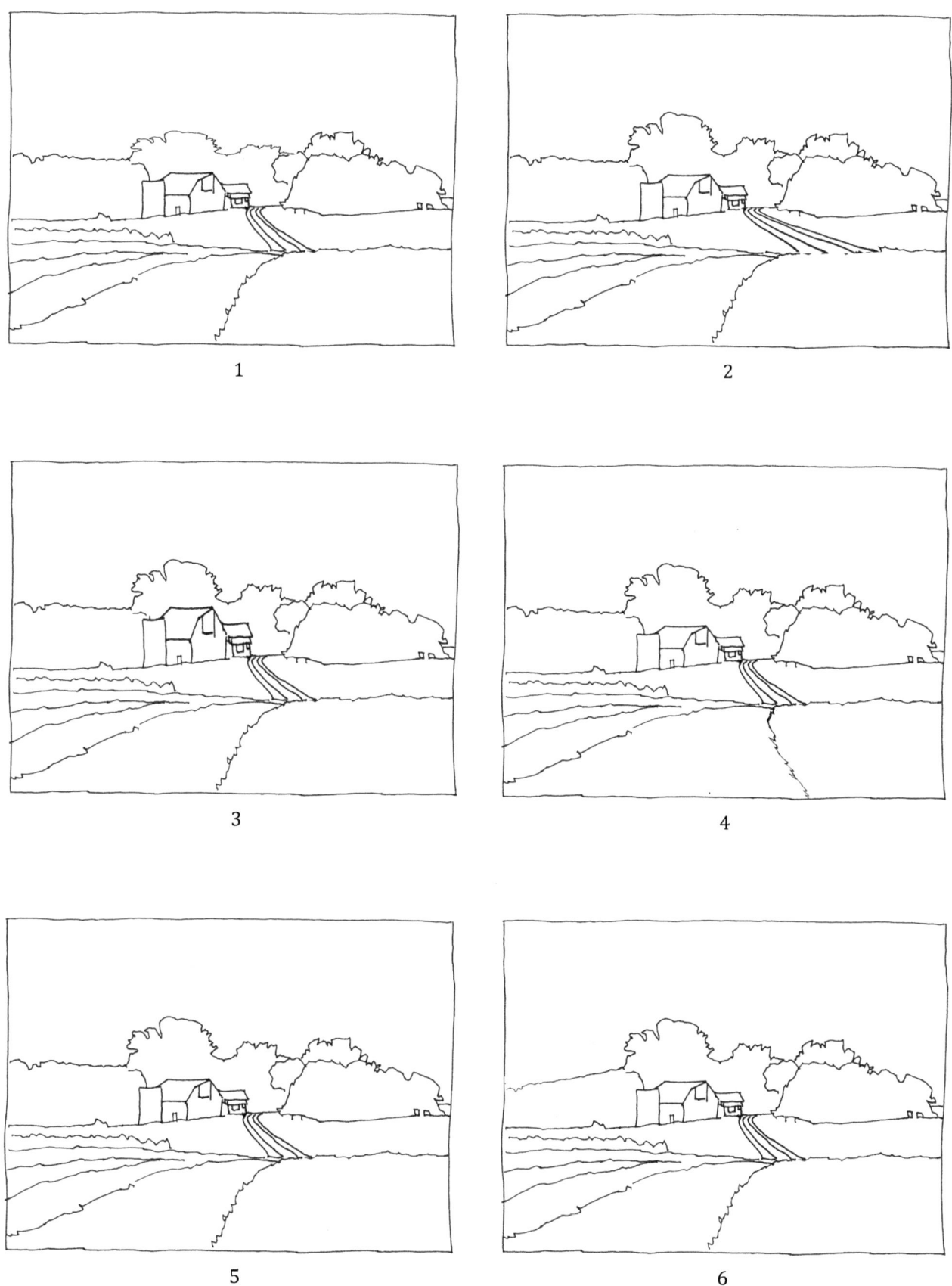

1

2

3

4

5

6

Using a pencil, draw the outline of the elephant in the bottom grid exactly as it is in the top. Pay attention to how the lines fit into the individual boxes formed by the grid and make your lines fit in the same way. Avoid thinking you're "drawing an elephant." Your task will seem easier if you concentrate on just drawing a bunch of lines that need to fit precisely into a gridded box.

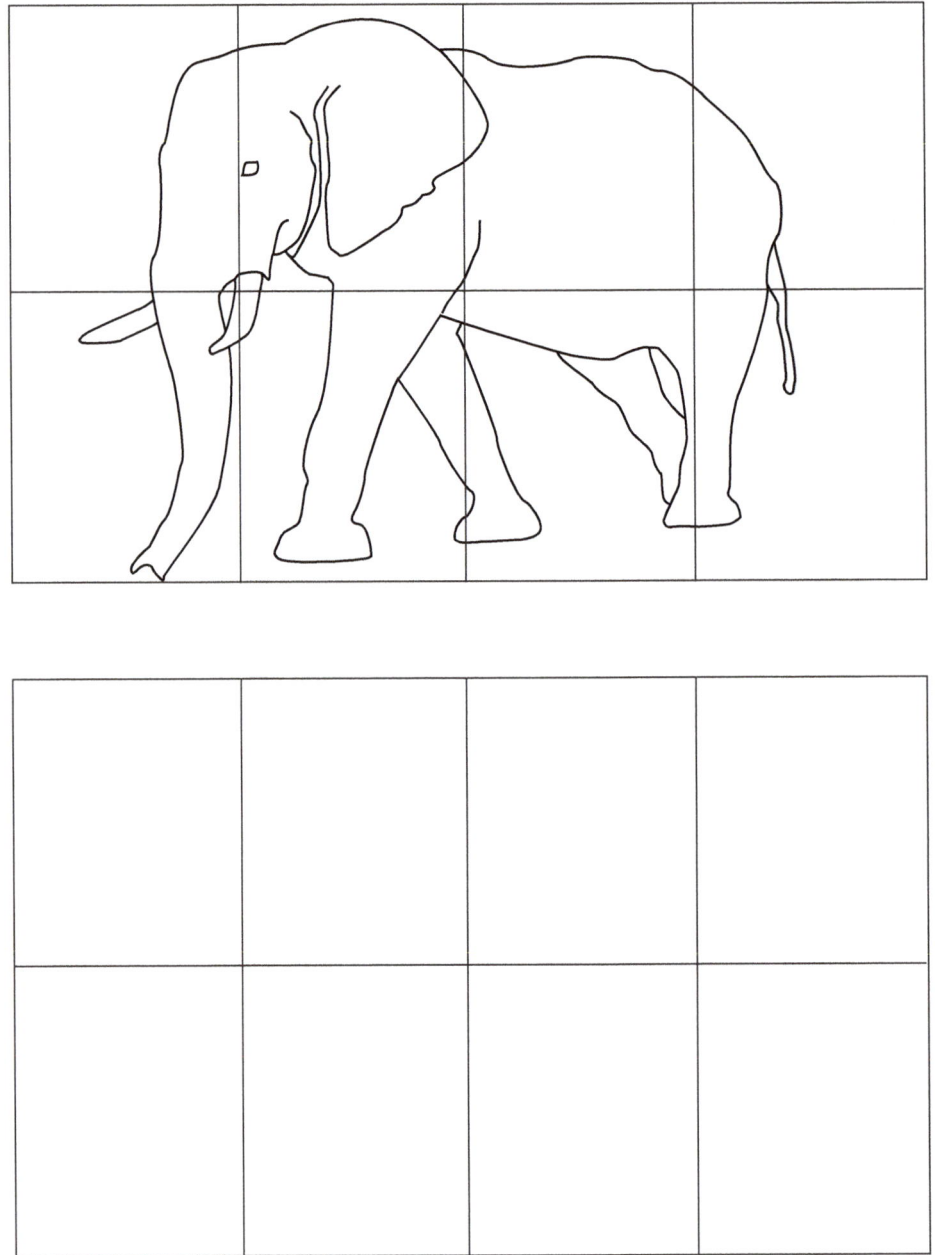

Up to this point, you've been on the lookout for differences in photos and drawings but in this exercise, it's changes that have been made to a graphic design. Compare the two invitations below. See if you can find the 15 changes that have been made to the invitation on the right. This exercise is one of the most difficult. Be a sleuth and don't give up.

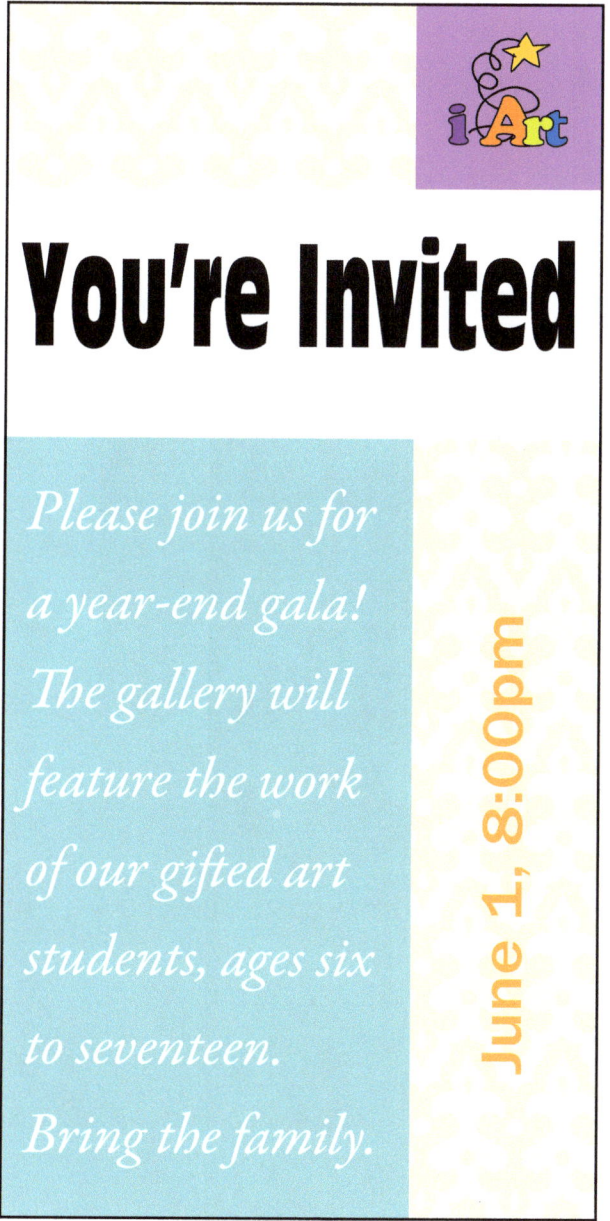

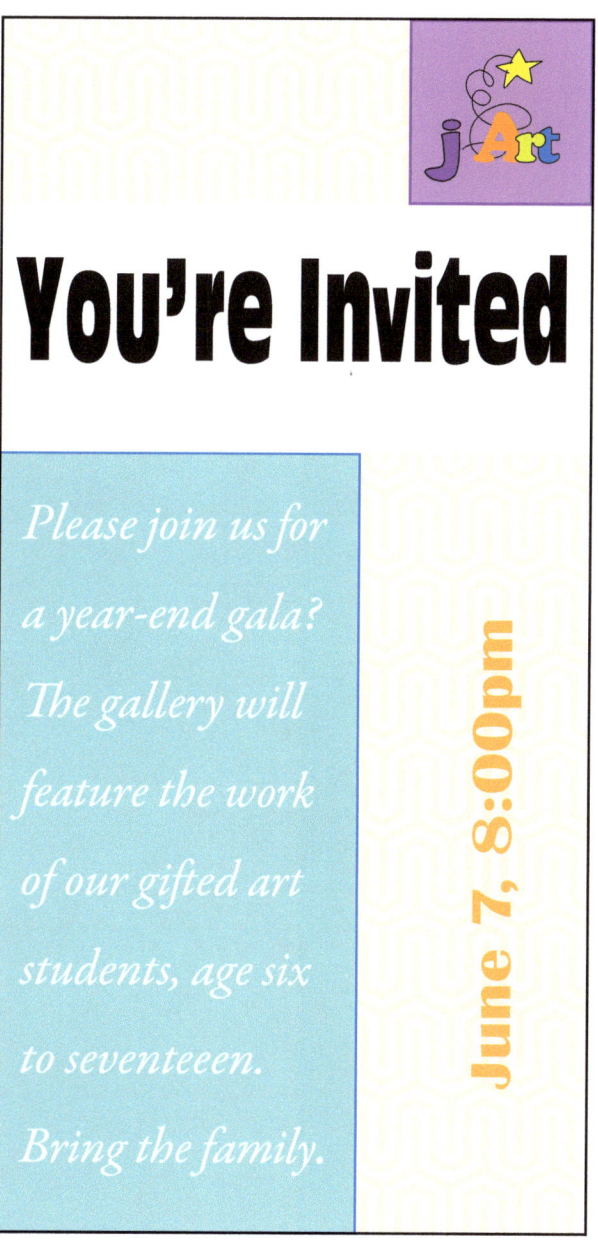

Carefully compare *photo 1* with *photo 2*. There are ten differences in *photo 2*. Most are not obvious, in fact some are barely noticeable. Don't get discouraged if you don't see them all right away. Take your time and study the two photos. Pay attention to colors. If this one is too hard, go on to another rather than just looking up the answer. You'll get better as you go and you can return to it later on. Hang in there with the struggle. That discomfort is a sign you're growing. Don't clutter your mind by trying to keep a mental list of the differences you find. Write them down on separate sheet of paper.

photo 1

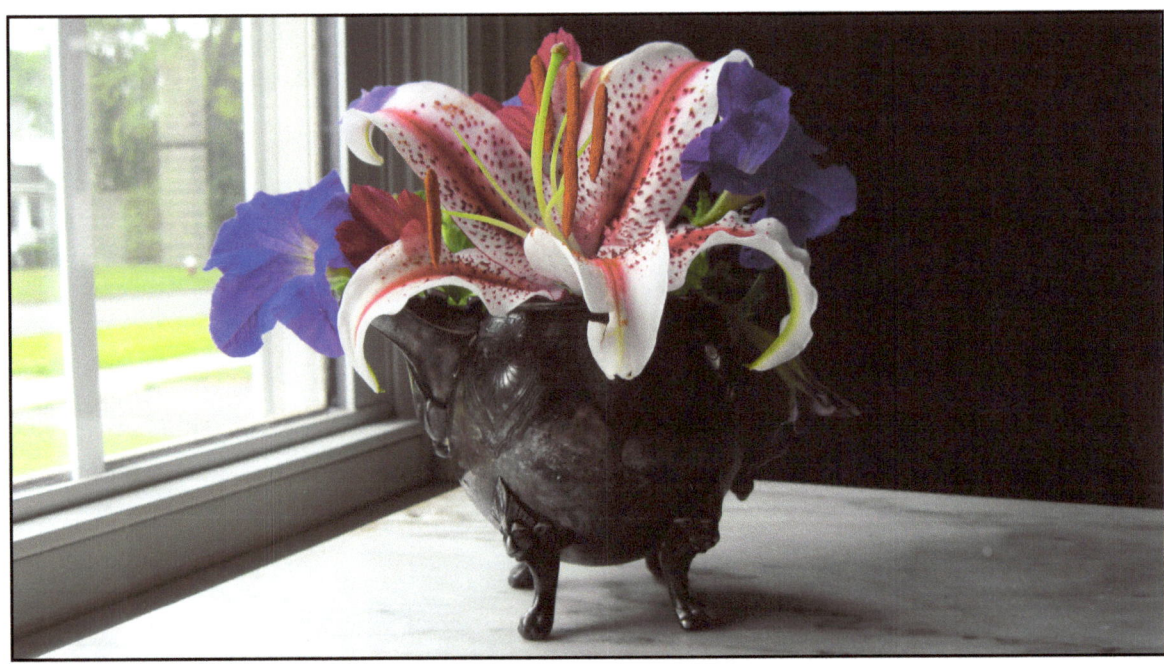

photo 2

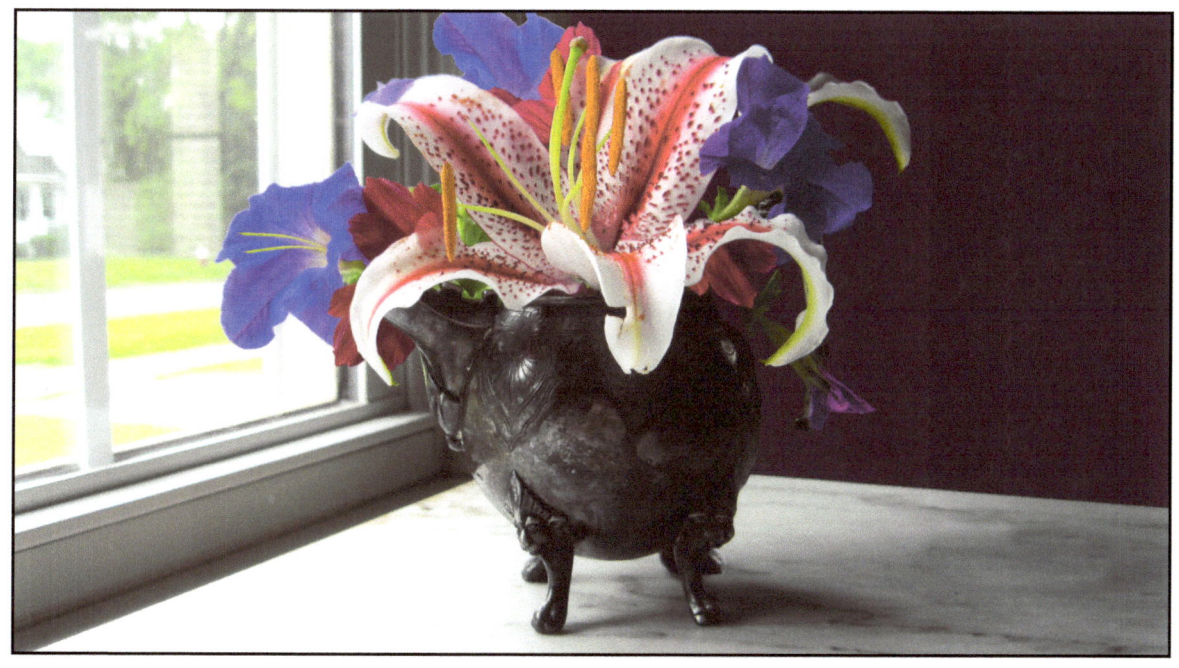

Draw the dinosaur in the bottom grid exactly as it is in the top grid. Make sure your lines fit the boxes in precisely the same way, paying close attention to how close lines are to edges or where lines cross the grid. When you're done, go back and check each box separately to see how well it matches and make any corrections to your drawing. Use pencil rather than pen so you can erase if necessary.

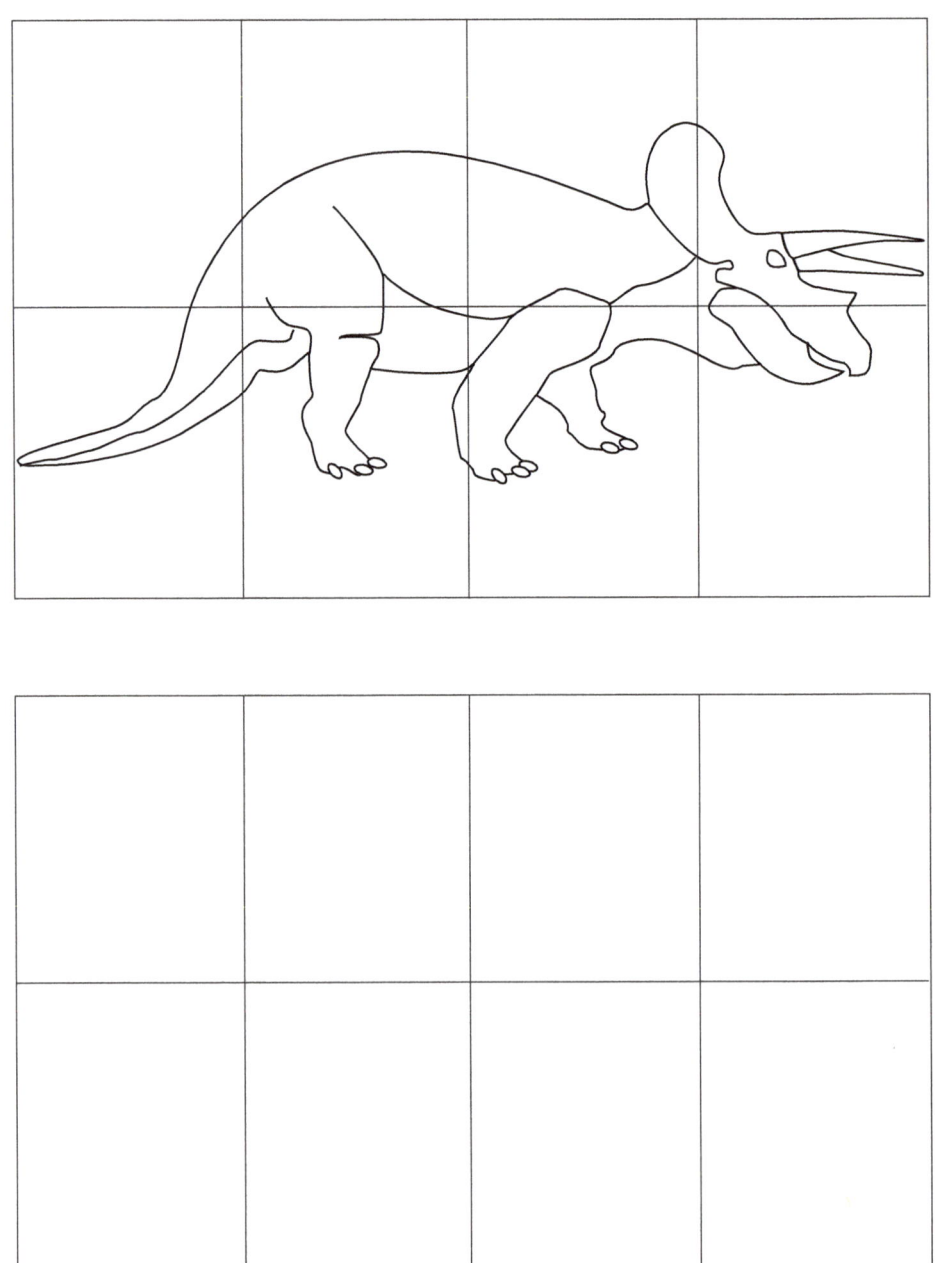

Draw the other side of this symmetrical vase. Use the left side as a guide for drawing the right side. Pay careful attention to how the lines fit the boxes and try to make yours fit in the same way. Notice how close lines come to edges and where the lines curve or touch. Remember this is a mirror image so you must draw the opposite side like you flipped the image over.

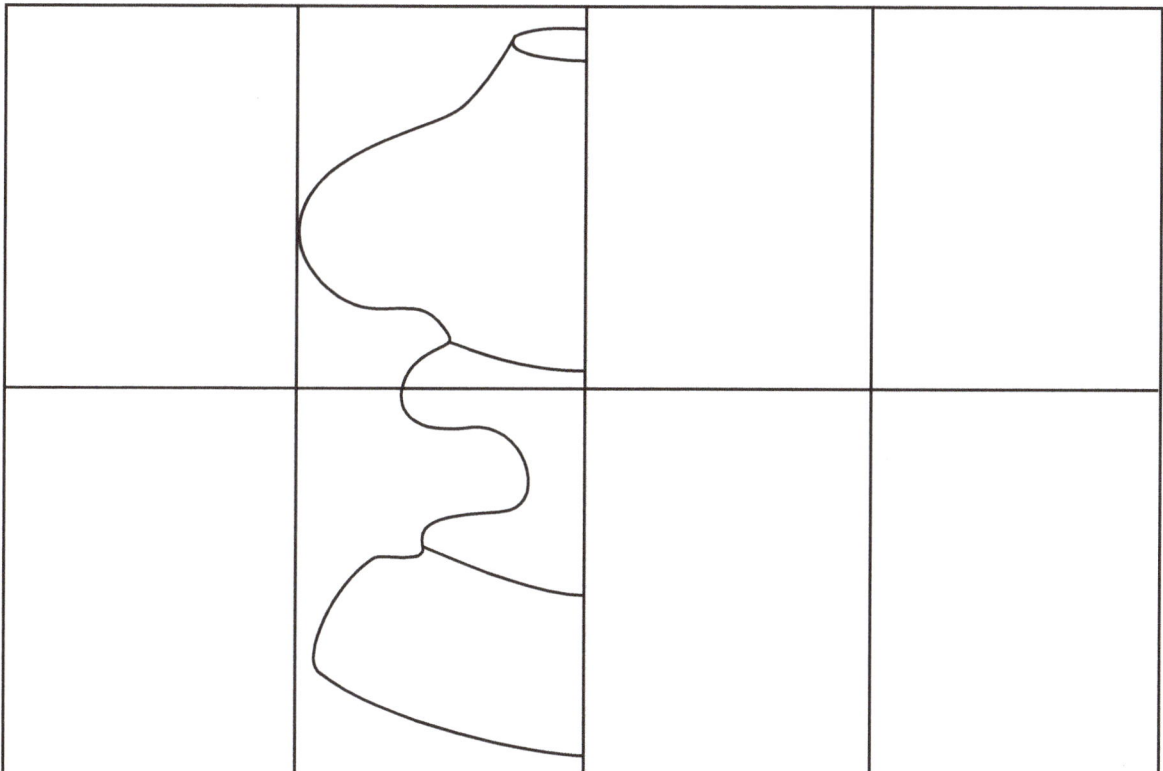

The silhouette in the red box is the one to match. There are two others that are the same. All the remaining silhouettes have been altered in small ways so take your time and observe carefully.

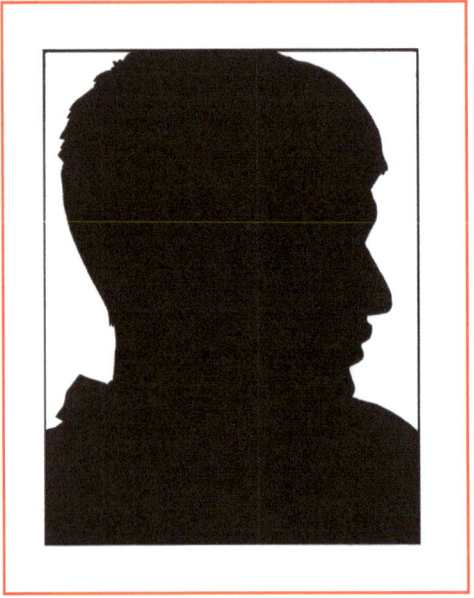

1

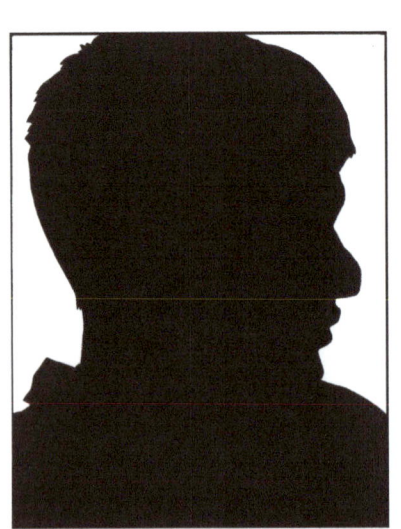

2

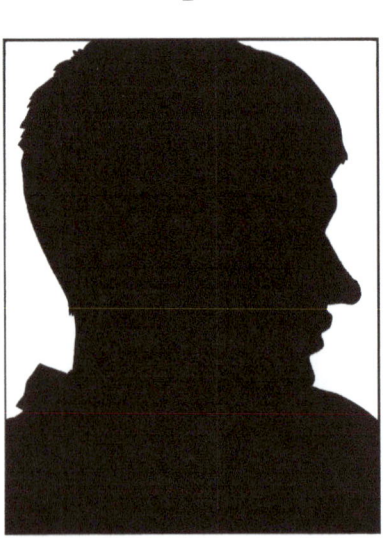

3

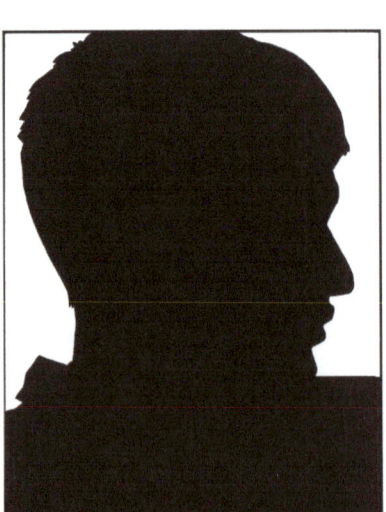

4 5 6

7 8 9

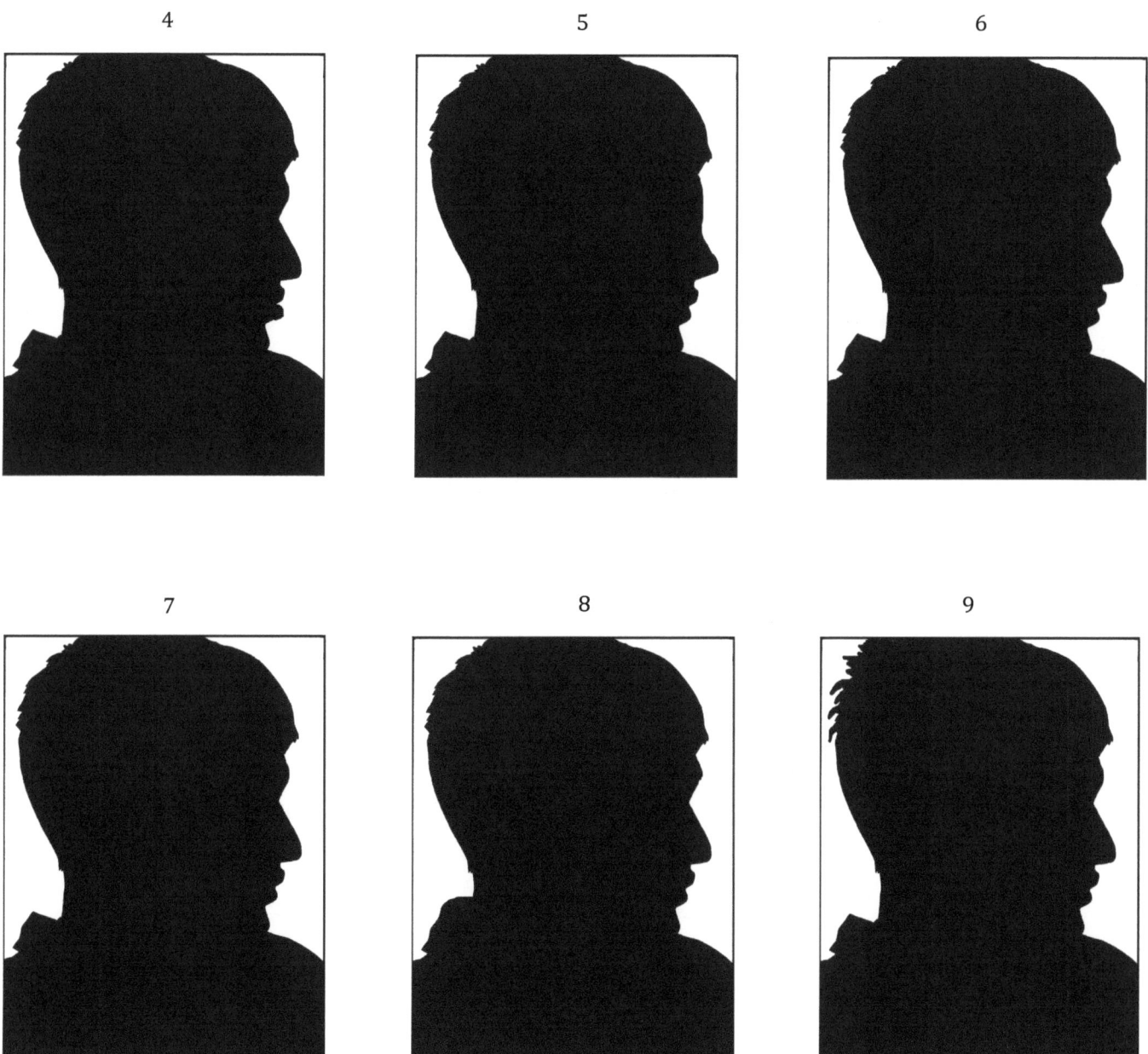

As you compare *drawing 1* with *drawing 2*, you should notice that there are parts missing in *drawing 2*. Using a pencil so you can erase if you need to, draw in the lines that are missing in *drawing 2*. Make sure they're in the right place but also that they're as close to the same kind of lines as you can make them. Try to copy lines exactly. If you get it wrong the first time, you'll know it because it will look wrong. Just erase it and try again. Slow down and look from one to the other over and over. Don't waste your time doing a "sort of right" job. Get it as right as you can because the struggle will train your eye.

drawing 1

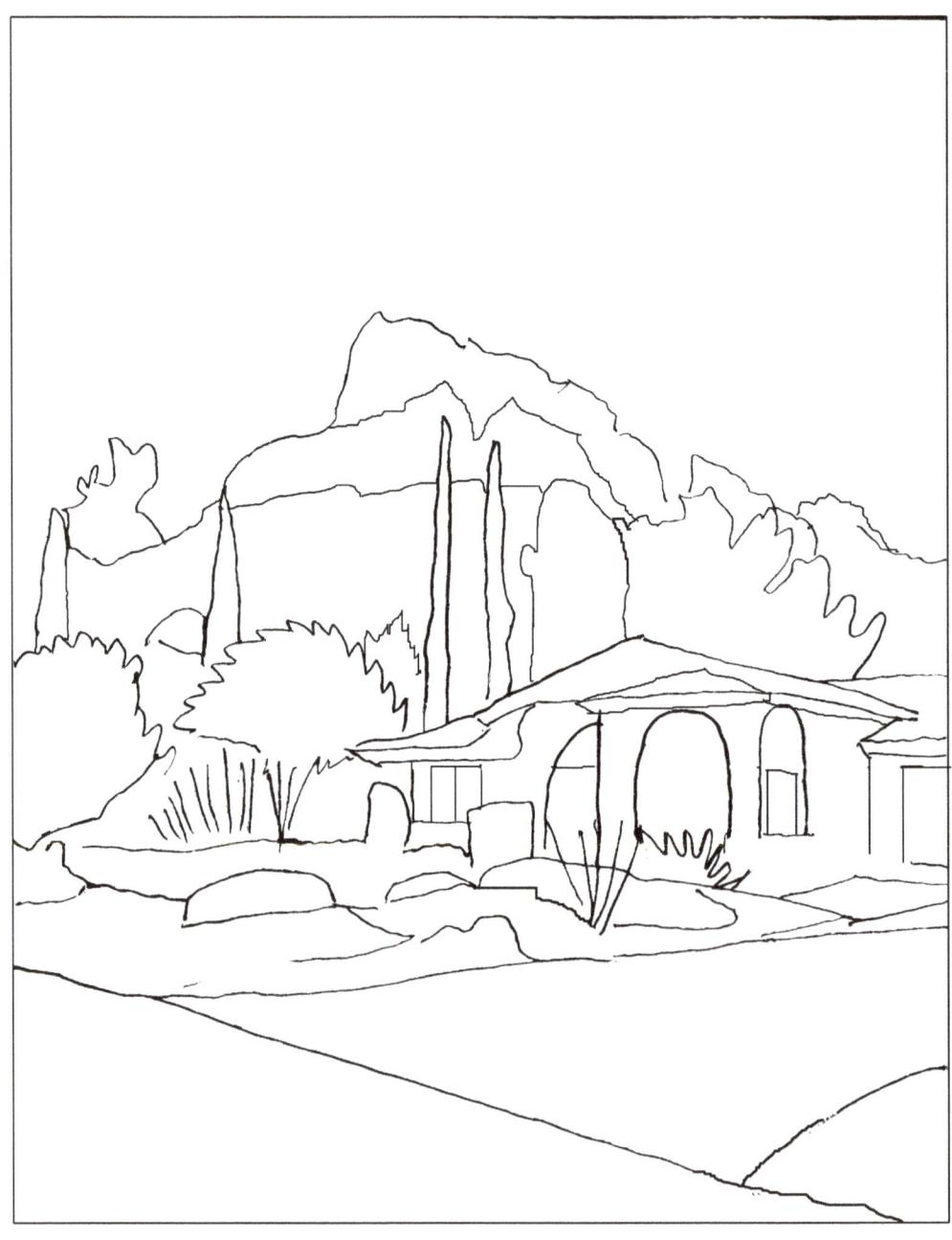

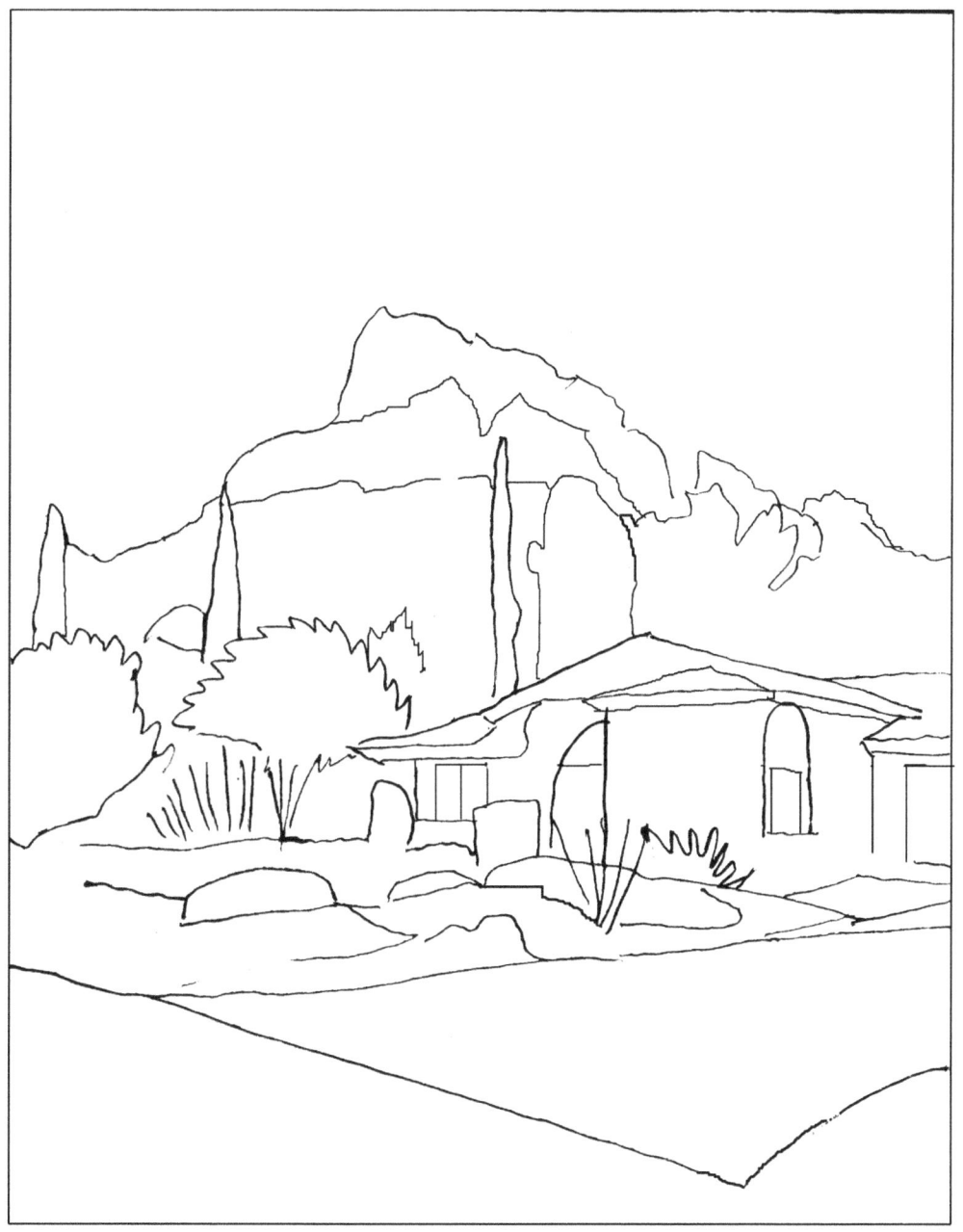

Do NOT draw the black parts! Ignore them. The white spaces are the subject matter in this exercise. Using a pencil, very lightly draw in the shapes of the white spaces within the grid on the following page. Draw smooth lines instead of trying to replicate the jagged edges. Be careful to notice where lines should begin on the outer edges and how far in toward the center they meet. Use the red lines as guides to help you reproduce the spatial relationships. Pay attention to the angle and thickness of lines and the shapes of spaces. Try to develop your own little tricks to help you notice things. For example, look at how the spaces relate to each other. Ask yourself "what is directly below this particular shape I'm drawing", or "how does that line up with something else?" The more opportunities you give yourself to notice differences, the faster your artist eye will develop.

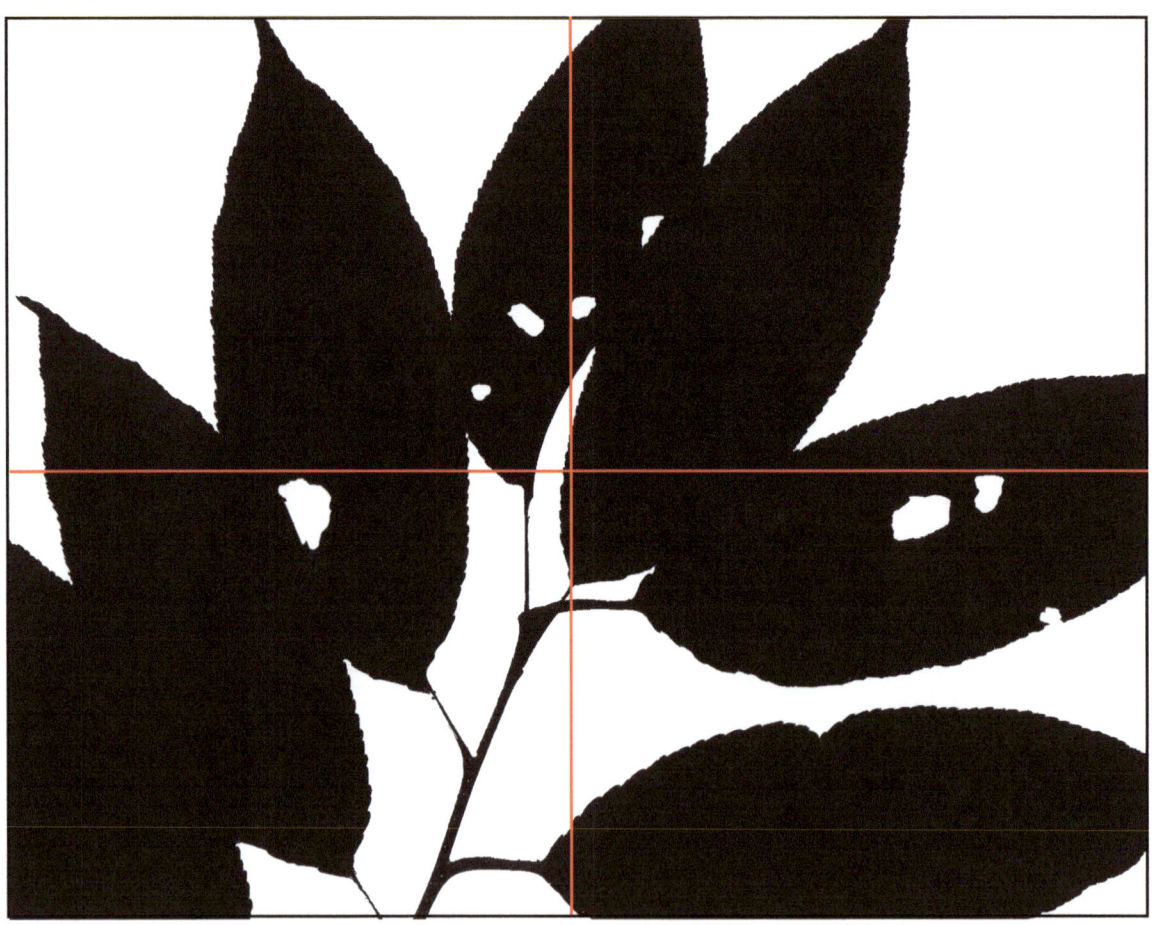

Answers

Page 6–Squirrel
1. two side holes in feeder filled with black
2. tray bottom colored black
3. extra line added above seed holes
4. line on feeder just above feet changed to zigzag
5. eye moved down
6. black center added to eye
7. extra leg added in back
8. bottom of tail smoothed out
9. back ear removed

Page 7–Dog
1. right ear tilted differently
2. bump on tail gone
3. eyes lower
4. far left paw curved on bottom instead of flat
5. tuft of fur on back leg removed
6. one less tuft of fur on chin
7. tuft of fur on front leg changed sides
8. tag removed
9. chin line added

Page 8-9–Ronnie the Rooster
1, 2, 4, 10, 19, 20, 22

Page 11–Bottles
1. first bottle on left slanted at different angle
2. second bottle has bigger cork
3. third bottle neck got shorter
4. fourth bottle oval design added
5. fourth bottle closer to fifth bottle
6. fourth bottle cork added
7. fifth bottle color changed
8. last bottle neck got taller

Page 12-13–Horse Puzzle
2, 3, 4, 6, 7, 9, 11, 12

Page 15–Pencils
1. yellow pencil changed to light purple
2. second purple pencil added
3. green pencil lead changed to lime green
4. second light blue pencil added
5. dark blue pencil tilted at different angle
6. red pencil turned light orange
7. short lime pencil added
8. black line added at bottom of jar
9. yellow ovals on jar got longer

10. white stripes turned light gray
11. end black stripe on right moved
12. black stripe farthest left eliminated
13. bump added to sides of jar

Page 16-17–Cartoon Crew
Skip: skin different color, mouth smaller
Harry: mouth flipped over, eyebrows gone
Bob: more hair
Anne: lips different color, ear added, eye color changed
Kent: glasses changed to red, bow tie added
Zeke: hat gone, added circle in eyes, added earring, hair color changed, nose different

Page 18–Truck
1. sky color is different
2. driver's hair color changed
3. door handle added
4. smoke added from smokestack
5. grassy hill darker green
7. front tire different pattern on sidewall
8. fatter black line on rim of tires
9. hubcap changed from orange to yellow
10. dirt added to scoop
11. man's shirt a different color
12. scoop rotated upwards
13. striped grill added to front of cab
14. fourth cloud added
15. tiny yellow circle added in center of wheels
16. panel under door changed to gray
17. cloud on right moved nearly off the picture
18. road color changed to violet
19. back bumper added to loader
20. circles on scoop changed to black
21. orange circle in center of wheels went black
22. black circle added to arm of scoop
23. smokestack changed color

Page 19–Rooster
1. comb on head last spike different
2. wattle (the thing under the beak) longer
3. beak longer
4. one feather in tail longer
5. entire wing moved left
6. feet different color
7. left leg moved farther left

8. eye color changed

page 21–Pelican
1. beak shorter
2. eye missing outer ring
3. back of head bigger
4. extra black feather added
5. tail changed shape
6. leg flipped over, points right
7. extra toe on foot
8. fluff on stomach added
9. stomach under beak smaller
10. beak now smiling
11. beak turned yellow
12. eyebrow added

Page 22-23–Eggs
1. small hole in center brown egg
2. extra white egg added to bowl
3 background color got lighter
4. bowl of eggs enlarged so view of right side of
   bowl gone also part of table that showed behind
   bowl on right no longer seen
5. extra brown egg added on table
6. table changed color
7. shadow removed below egg on table
8. design added to bowl
9 extra brown egg added to bowl
10. two original eggs on table got slightly larger
11. table got expanded so less of wall shows

Page 24–Jars and Apples
4 & 6

Page 25–Lines
7 & 12

Page 27–Vegetables
1. added carrot on right behind red onion
2. center part of red pepper changed color
3. small yellow pepper in front moved far left
4. green pepper changed to yellow
5. cucumber on left slants down more
6. some of green beans changed to yellow
7. mushroom on right behind tomato moved to far
   left side front
8. tomato far right changed to green
9. potato behind tomato far right got darker brown

10. extra red onion added behind on left
11. one of three red potatoes on left deleted
12. small yellow pepper to left of green pepper
    changed color
13. mushroom added in front of beans
14. potato added center behind carrot

Page 28–Gazelles
1,2,3,8,12,16

Page 29–Giraffes
2

Page 30-31–Tea Cup
1. cup larger
2. third piece of toast added
3. lemon went from yellow to orange
4. middle white stripes in napkin changed to yellow
5. tea a darker brown
6. background color changed
7. shadow under cup removed
8. bite taken out of strawberry in cup design
9. chip on rim of cup
10. daisy flower missing on right side of saucer

Page 33–Butterflies
10

Page 36-37–Flower Collage
2, 5, 7, 10, 12, 19, 27

Page 38-39–Kids in a Rowboat
1. color of tree on far right greener
2. oar on left missing
3. number on boat changed
4. row of trees taller and covers more of sky
5. boat moved from left to middle
6. girl's hair redder
7. the boy's shirt changed color
8. couple in a canoe added on left
9. geese added on right
10 girls shirt in reflection changed color
11. tree and street added to back row of trees
12. lighter colored reeds along shore moved right

Page 40-41–Farm
5

Page 43–Invitation
1. white text smaller
2. star in logo went from gold to yellow
3. peachy background pattern different
4. extra "e" was added to "seventeen"
5. font used in date and time changed
6. "i" in logo changed to "j"
7. in white text–exclamation point (!) after "gala" changed to question mark (?)
8. dark blue line added around blue box
9. black squiggle in logo got skinnier
10. blue box got thinner so doesn't come as close to date & time
11. line added around purple box
12. orange "A" in logo lost black outline
13. apostrophe in "You're" different
14. "v" in "Invited" smaller than rest of letters
15. in date-"1" changed to "7"
16. in white text–the s in "ages" was deleted

Page 44-45–Flowers in the Window
1. flower bud farthest right in back changed from purple to magenta
2. stamens on white flower changed color
3. another white petal added back right
4. background went from black to dark maroon
5. extra purple flower added at top
6. extra magenta flower added on right under white petal
7. back foot of vase on right showing more
8. handle of pitcher on right deleted
9. magenta petal added behind pitcher spout on left
10. stamens added to purple flower far left

Page 48-49–Silhouettes
6 & 7

www.ingramcontent.com/pod-product-compliance
Lightning Source LLC
Chambersburg PA
CBHW050809180526
45159CB00004B/1605